मूलाधारे कुण्डलिनी भुजगाकाररूपिणी ।
तत्र तिष्ठति जीवात्मा प्रदीपकलिकाकृतिः ।
ध्यायेत्तेजोमयं ब्रह्म तेजोध्यानं परात्परम् ॥ १६ ॥

In the Mūlādhāra, Kuṇḍalinī lies in the form of a coiled serpent. The innate self dwells there like the flame of a lamp. Contemplation of this radiant light as the luminous Brahman is the transcendental meditation.

Gheraṇḍa Saṁhitā, v. 16

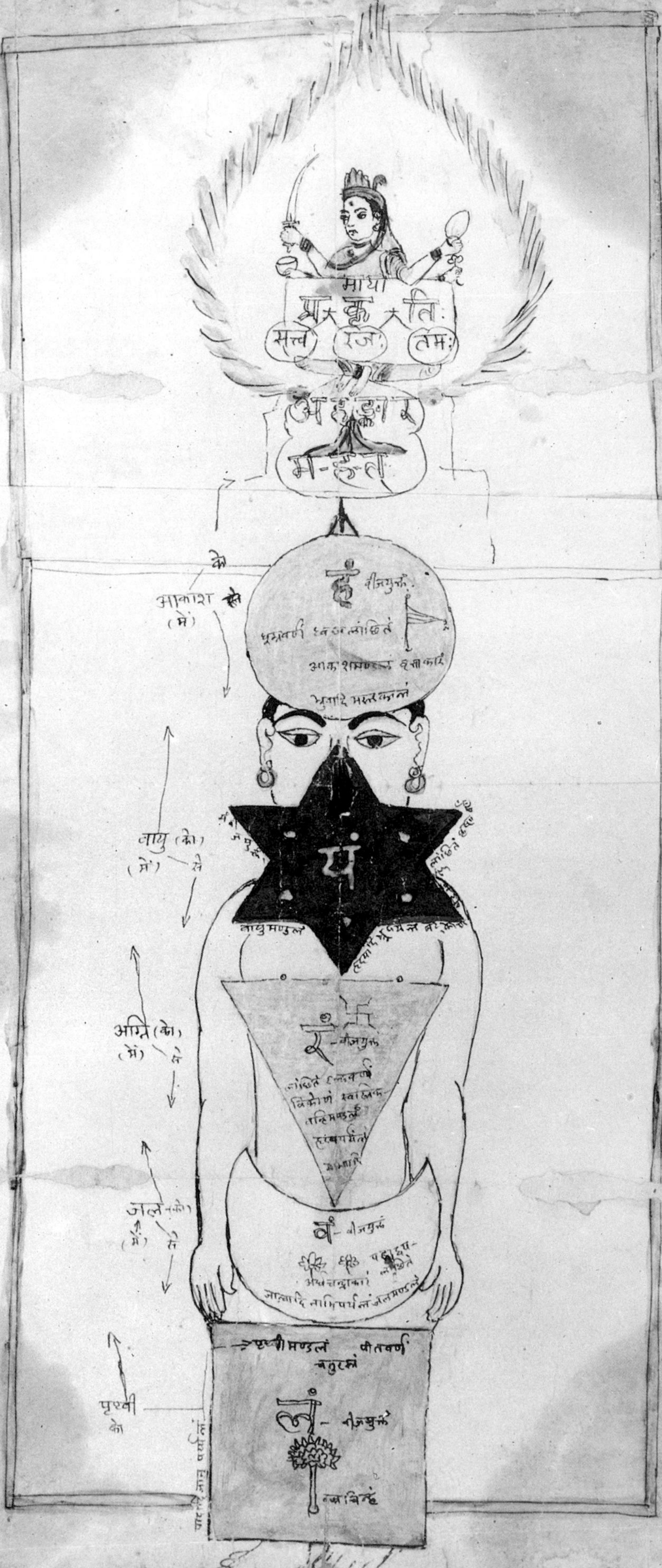
माया
प्रकृतिः
सत्त्व
रजः
तमः
अहङ्कार
महत्
आकाश
वायु (को)
(में) से
अग्नि (को)
(में) से
जल
(में) से
पृथ्वी
को

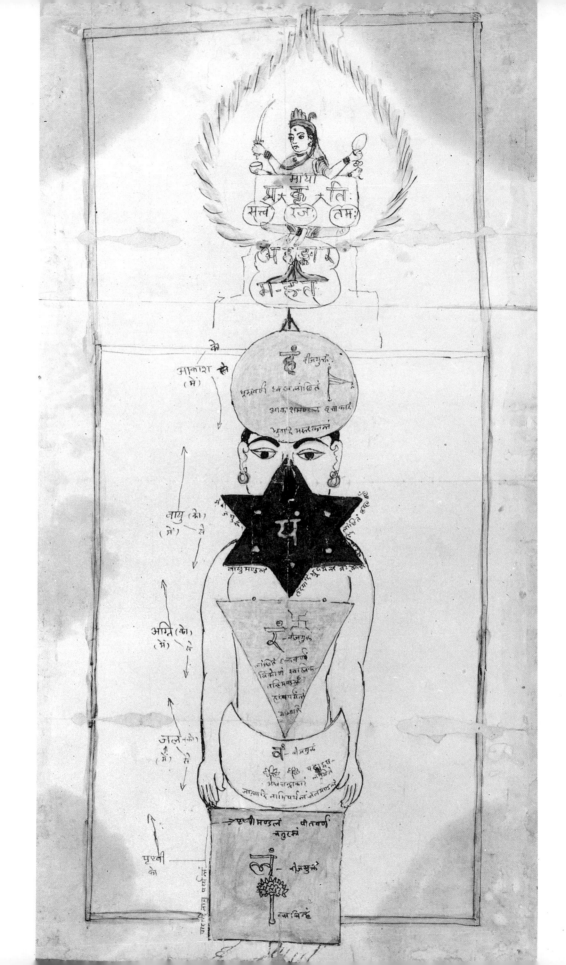

Ajit Mookerjee

KUNDALINI

The Arousal of the Inner Energy

DESTINY BOOKS
Rochester, Vermont

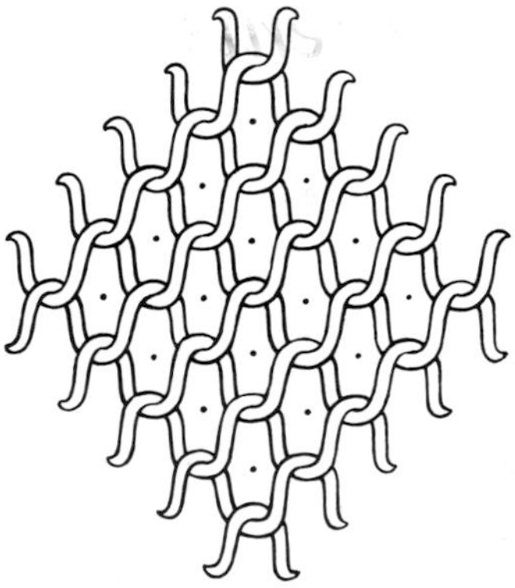

Frontispiece: The energy centres with (above) the full flowering of the female Kuṇḍalinī energy. Rajasthan, c. 1900, ink and colour on paper

Copyright page : Ancient Dravidian symbol of the interweaving psychic energies (Kolam), South India

Destiny Books
Park Street
Rochester, Vermont 05767
www.InnerTraditions.com

Third Edition 1986

Library of Congress Cataloging in Publication Data

Mookerjee, Ajit.
Kundalini, the arousal of the inner energy.
Bibliography : p. 101
Includes index.
1. Kundalini. I. Title.
BL1215.K8M66 1982 294.5'514 81-5466
ISBN 0-89281-020-3 (pbk.) AACR2

10 9 8

Contents

Preface

Human experience owes to Tantra the discovery and location of the centres of psychic energy, chakras, in the subtle or astral body. Kuṇḍalinī Śakti, coiled and dormant cosmic energy, is at the same time the supreme force in the human organism. Every individual is a manifestation of that energy, and the universe around us is the outcome of the same consciousness, ever revealing itself in various modes. The passage of the awakened Kuṇḍalinī through the various chakras is the subject of a unique branch of tantric esoteric knowledge whose goal is the merging of the Kuṇḍalinī energy with cosmic consciousness, so that one may realize one's real self, ultimately unfolding the mysteries of the whole universe.

Kuṇḍalinī-yoga is an experience of the actualization of human potentialities. A deeper understanding of the awakening of this cosmic energy can only be felt when one decides to become actively involved in it. As Dr B. Bhattacharyya remarks: 'Whenever in the future, man awakens to the necessity of psychic development, spiritual advancement, or of stimulating his latent magical faculties, all eyes must turn towards this branch of Sanskrit literature, and to those few Yogins India still possesses, for the most minute, thorough, accurate, easy and practical system of psychic exercises ever conceived by man in any country or at any time.'

The Kuṇḍalinī awakening or rebirth-process has been studied both from the classical and clinical point of view. In this study, my special thanks are due to Dr Lee Sannella, Chief of Clinical Services of the Kuṇḍalinī Clinic, whose permission to use the clinical findings has been very useful. I am grateful to Dick Price and Stanislav and Christina Grof of the Esalen Institute, Big Sur, California, for providing me with opportunities to meet American researchers on kuṇḍalinī-yoga. I am also indebted to Madhu Khanna for her several suggestions and to Pria Devi for going through the manuscript.

A.M.

Nāga-bandha. The psychic energy symbolized by the serpent-form retained by being wound into a 'closed circuit'. Rajasthan, 18th century, ink and colour on paper

नीयं कुंडलिनी स्यान्सिंहूरव लीसर्षाकारं अथोमुखेनचाघि देवता कुहार

शिक्ति चलऋषि: कर्म क लाइ-द्दीपाएबंध: कामद्रूयेमंडलकामासा

री गर्भे वासस्थाने जठराघ्नि स्थानेबाऊ येयभट नश्या

नीयो गर्भिसाधेय मायाकुंडि लिनी व्राका कामद्रू पाभि

वासिनी ॥ ॥

सधिष्ठानंद्वितीयं वलिंगस्थानेप्रतिष्ठिते पीनवलेर्ज्ञोज्जकमकारेस

मन्निते ९ तच्चवलादेवतायायत्रीषा कि:वरुण ऋषि: कामाघ्रिउज्वा

धारलौ स्थूलोदेहोजायरावस्था वैखरी वाक् ऋग्वेदआयोलिंगगलाभू

कासायुज्यमोहोहं सोवाहनं षट्र लानि वद्मात्रा चंभमयरंलंब्लनमात्रा

बाका ९ कादा २ तेजसी ३ ह्लादा ४ मि छुना ५ देवरला ६ अज्जया न

पसहस्रालि १००० यष्टिकानि ९६ पलानि ८० अक्षरालि ८० सोहेभ

वेपूज येत् गंधारिकंचरध्यान् ॥ ॥ ॥

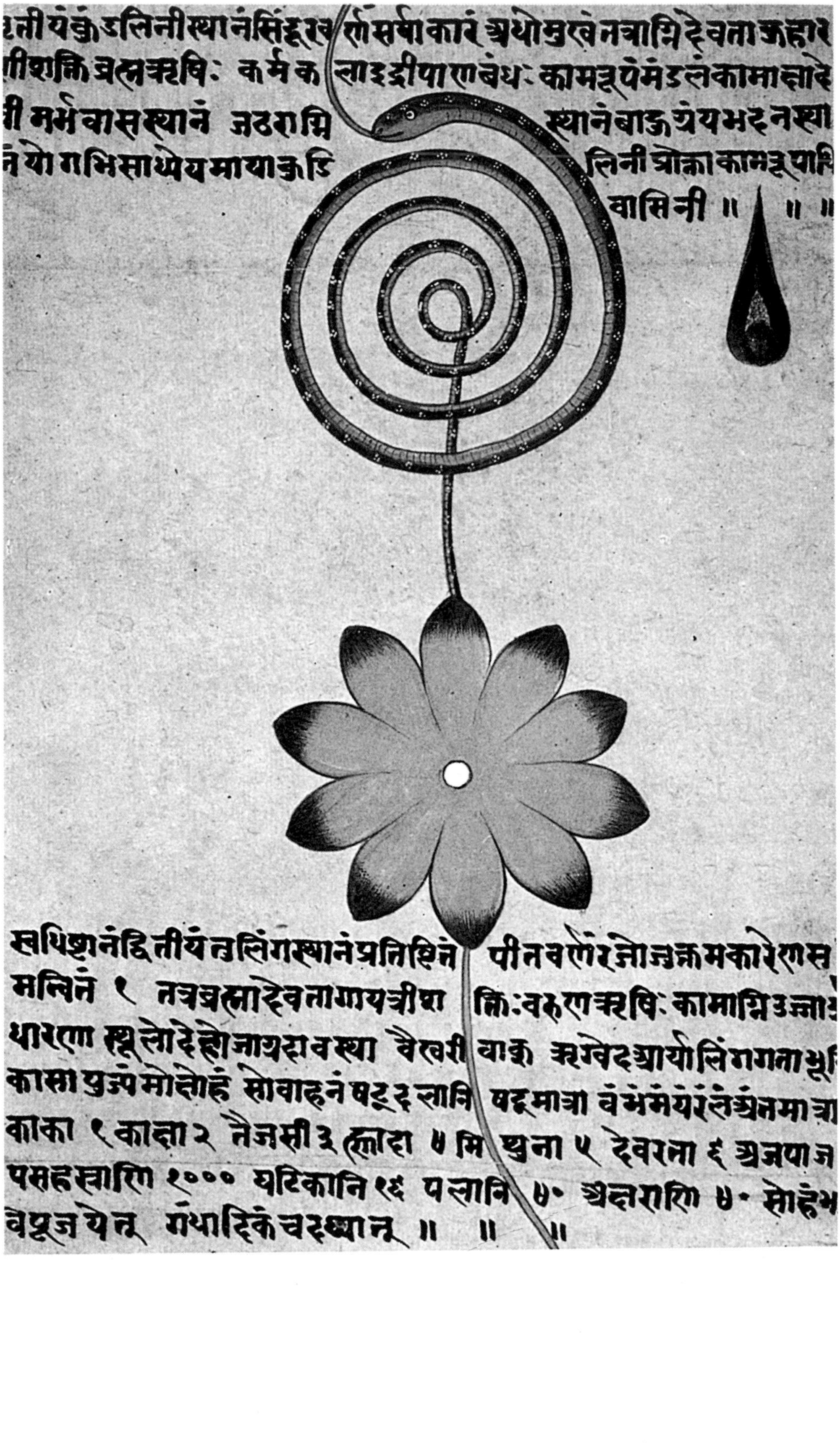

1
The Tantric Concept

The Kuṇḍalinī, in the form of latency,
is coiled like a serpent. One who impels
this Śakti to move will attain liberation.

Haṭhayoga-pradīpikā, Chap. 3, v. 108

Liberation while living is considered in Indian life to be the highest experience – a fusion of the individual with the universal. The individual manifestation is like a spark of the cosmos, as the human organism, the microcosm, parallels everything in the macrocosm. The complete drama of the universe is repeated here, in this very body. The whole body with its biological and psychological processes becomes an instrument through which the cosmic power reveals itself. According to tantric principles, all that exists in the universe must also exist in the individual body. If we can analyse one human being, we shall be able to analyse the entire universe, because it is believed that all is built on the same plane. The purpose is to search for the whole truth within, so that one may realize one's inner self, unfolding the basic reality of the universe.

The point of connection is yoga, for yoga is the 'way'. In bhakti-yoga, union takes place through love and devotion; rāja-yoga is the path of realization through meditation; karma-yoga is the way of salvation through works; jñāna-yoga leads to union through discernment, while haṭha-yoga develops psychosomatic forces towards the ultimate goal.

An important tantric contribution to consciousness-expanding experience is kuṇḍalinī-yoga. The Sanskrit word *kuṇḍalinī* means 'coiled-up'. The coiled Kuṇḍalinī is the female energy existing in latent form, not only in every human being but in every atom of the universe. It may frequently happen that an individual's Kuṇḍalinī energy lies dormant throughout his or her entire lifetime and he or she is unaware of its existence. The object of the tantric practice of kuṇḍalinī-yoga is to awaken this cosmic energy and cause it to unite with Śiva, the Pure Consciousness pervading the whole universe.

Ascent of the female energy, Kuṇḍalinī. Detail of scroll painting, Kangra School, c. 18th century, gouache on paper

Mūlādhāra chakra, the root chakra at the base of the spine, where the unawakened Kuṇḍalinī lies coiled around the Svayaṁbhu-liṅga

The Kuṇḍalinī Śakti or 'coiled feminine energy' is the vast potential of psychic energy, the body's most powerful thermal current. The arousal of Kuṇḍalinī is not unique to tantric practice, but forms the basis of all yogic disciplines, and every genuine spiritual experience may be considered a flowering of this physio-nuclear energy. Even music and dance can arouse the Kuṇḍalinī's dormant force and direct it to higher planes, until its perfect unfolding and our conscious awareness of its presence within us is realized.

The *Ṣaṭcakra-nirūpaṇa* (v. 3) describes Kuṇḍalinī almost tenderly, saying: 'She is beautiful as a chain of lightning and fine as a [lotus] fibre, and shines in the minds of the sages. She is extremely subtle, the awakener of pure knowledge, the embodiment of bliss, whose true nature is pure consciousness.' Kuṇḍalinī is described as 'pure consciousness' in another text, the *Mahānirvāṇa Tantra* (5. 19) which states that Kuṇḍalinī is primal Prakṛiti or Nature, who is none other than *Cit-śakti* or Pure Consciousness. The *Sāradātilaka* (1.13–14) describes Kuṇḍalinī as Śabda-brahmamayī (the female counterpart of Śiva as Śabda-brahman, the source of cosmic sound) in the form of the mantra, or nuclear sound-syllable, the proximate cause of manifestation.

The sounds of the Sanskrit alphabet are not mere verbal utterance, but are self-subsisting, embodying all potentialities. According to the *Kāmadhenu Tantra* (p. 3), the left side of the Sanskrit letter *ka* (क) forms a triangle whose upper-left line symbolizes Brahmā, right-vertical line Vishṇu and lower-left line Rudra, while in the coiled extension in front, Kuṇḍalinī lies latent.

When this Kuṇḍalinī Śakti moves to manifest itself, it becomes dynamic. The one Consciousness is polarized into static (Śiva) and dynamic (Śakti) aspects for the purpose of manifestation. Kuṇḍalinī-yoga is the resolution of this duality into unity again.

In the concept of the *Yoga Kuṇḍalinī Upanishad* (1.82):

> *The divine power,*
> *Kuṇḍalinī, shines*
> *like the stem of a young lotus;*
> *like a snake, coiled round upon herself,*
> *she holds her tail in her mouth*
> *and lies resting half asleep*
> *at the base of the body.*

The static, unmanifested Kuṇḍalinī is symbolized by a serpent coiled into three and a half circles, with its tail in its mouth, and spiralling around the central axis or Svayaṁbhu-liṅga at the base of the spine. When the Kuṇḍalinī Śakti (Power Consciousness) is

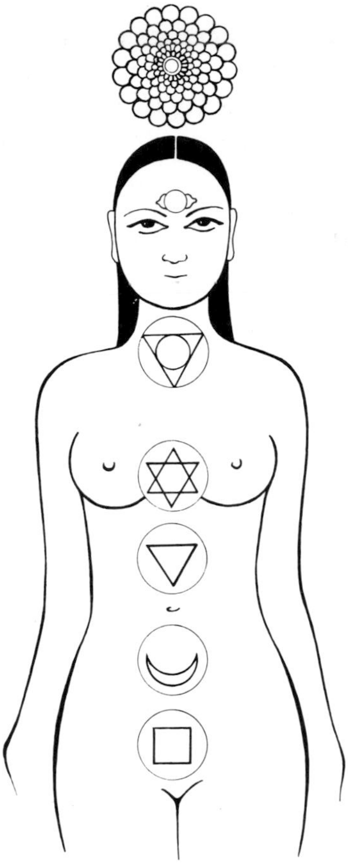

Psychic centres in the etheric body of the human organism

ready to unfold, she ascends to unite above the crown of the head with Śiva (Pure Consciousness), whose manifest energy she is, through the psychic centres, the chakras (or cakras), that lie along the axis of the spine as consciousness potentials. All the chakras are to be understood as situated, not in the gross body, but in the subtle or etheric body. Repositories of psychic energies, they govern the whole condition of being.

Tantras commonly mention six principal holistically organized centres of consciousness, though the number varies from text to text. Starting from the base of the spine, these centres are known as Mūlādhāra, Svādhisthāna (around the prostatic plexus), Maṇipūra (around the navel), Anāhata (near the heart), Viśuddha (behind the throat), and Ājñā (between the eyebrows). Sahasrāra, the seventh, transcendent chakra, is situated four-fingers' breadth above the top of the head. The Sahasrāra chakra is said to be the region of Śiva, Pure Consciousness, while the Mūlādhāra chakra is the seat of Śakti, whose form here is Kuṇḍalinī. Through certain prescribed disciplines the Kuṇḍalinī Śakti rises through the psychic centres until it reaches its full flowering – that is, fusion with the

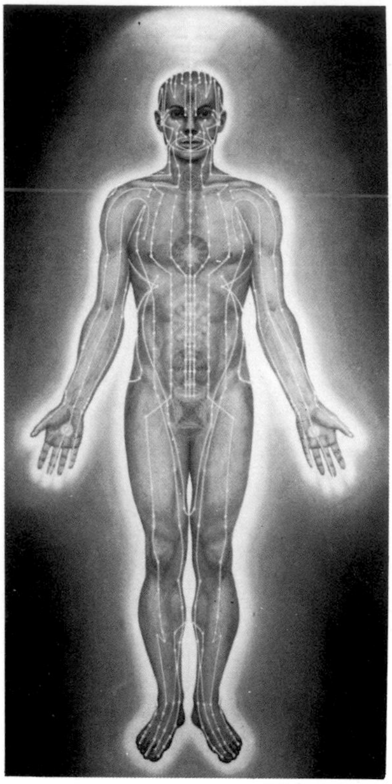

A Western representation of the etheric body with its chakras and acupuncture meridians (Alex Grey, contemporary)

The chakras in the etheric body of the yogi, and the ascending planes of Kuṇḍalinī experience. Rajasthan, c. 18th century, gouache on paper

Absolute in Sahasrāra as Kula-kuṇḍalinī, generating bliss-consciousness (ānanda) from the union of Śiva-Śakti.

Tantrikas regard the human organism as a capsule of the whole. 'He who realizes the truth of the body can then come to know the truth of the universe' (*Ratnasāra*). The adept accepts this with an almost existential awareness. The psychic and physical organisms are interdependent, since each makes the other possible. The forces governing the cosmos on the macro-level govern the individual on the micro-level. Life is one, and all its forms are interrelated in a vastly complicated but inseparable whole. The underlying unity becomes a bridge between the microcosm and the macrocosm. 'The human body, like the electro-magnetic bodies of the sun or the earth, has with our present knowledge expanded beyond its physical confines, revealing the subtle human faculties beyond the five senses: the auras of the 'aetheric' body, and its organs – the 'chakras' – of religious tradition, the streams of 'qi' energy which the acupuncturist traces – all of which emanations parallel and fuse with the energy rhythms of our planet, and beyond.'[1]

Each human being has an 'etheric double', a subtle or sūkśma body. Besides the 'gross' body (sthūla śarīra), there are the 'subtle' body (liṅga or sūkśma śarīra) and the 'causal' body (kāraṇa śarīra). In the Tantras, the human body is regarded as made up of five envelopes or cosmic folds, the sheaths or kośas, creating layers of decreasing density. The physical metabolism is known as the Annamaya-kośa (food-formed sheath) of the gross body; more subtle is the sheath of circulatory vital air, the Prāṇamaya-kośa; the third and fourth sheaths, more subtle still, are the cognitive and discriminatory processes, the Manomaya and Vijñānamaya (mind and intelligence sheaths) of the subtle body. The final sheath, Ānandamaya, the most subtle of all, is identified with man's extraordinary capacity for joy (the bliss consciousness), and belongs to the causal body.

The physical sheath of the body, Annamaya, is connected with three of the five elements – earth, water and fire – which are represented respectively in the Mūlādhāra, Svādhisthāna and Maṇipūra chakras. The Prāṇamaya sheath, bearing the universal life-force, Prāṇa, expresses itself through the air and ether elements which are represented in the Anāhata and Viśuddha chakras; the Manomaya and Vijñānamaya sheaths have the Ājñā chakra as their centre. It is the activation of the Ājñā chakra that gives the initiate inner vision, a simultaneous knowledge of things as they really are, as the 'third eye', cosmic consciousness, opens at this centre.

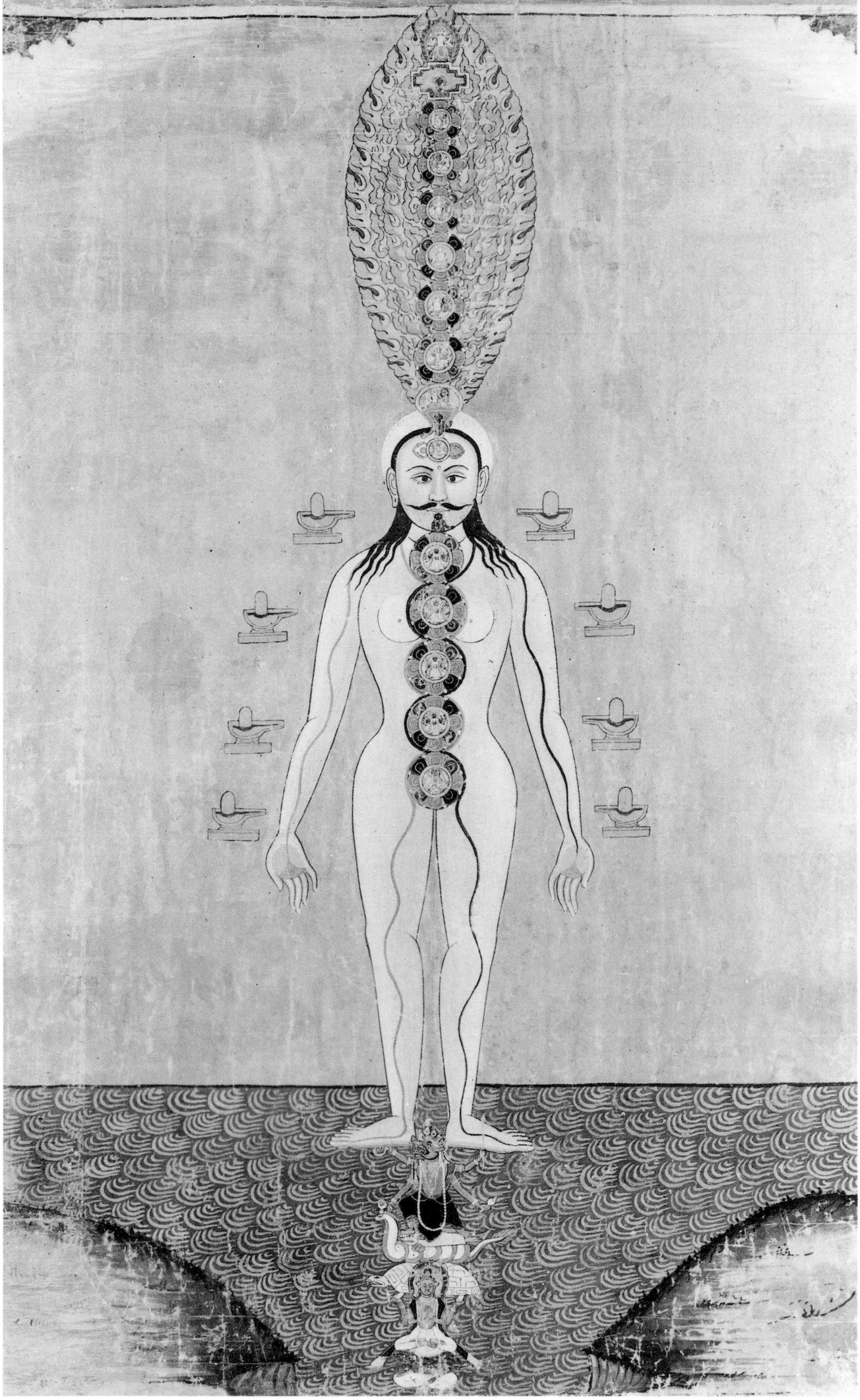

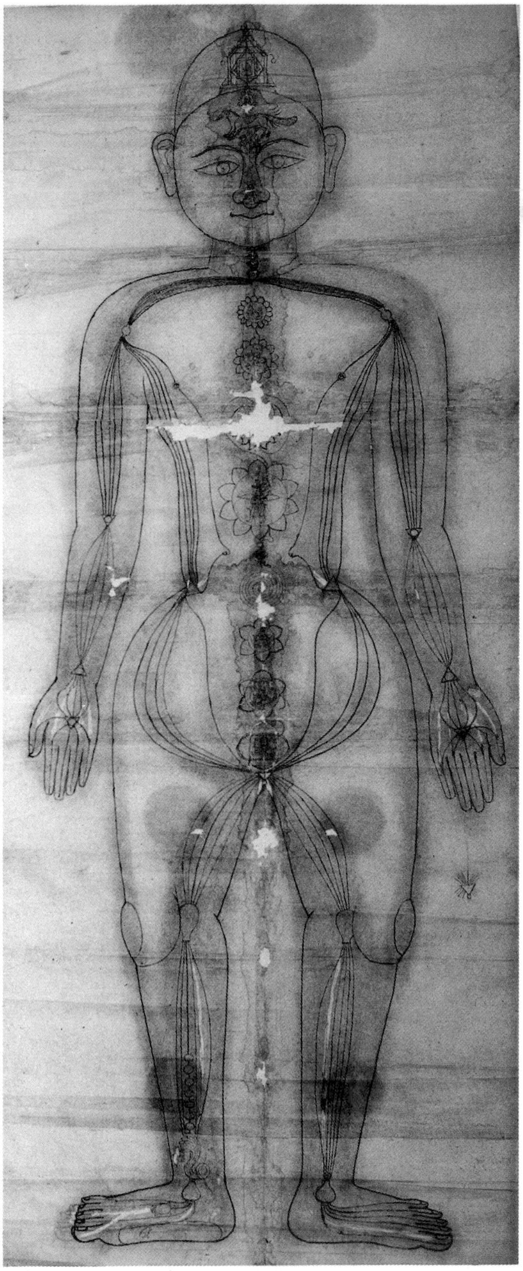

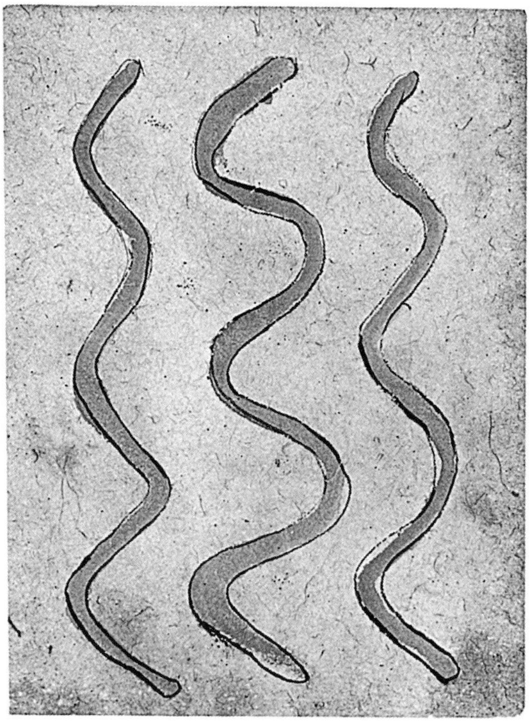

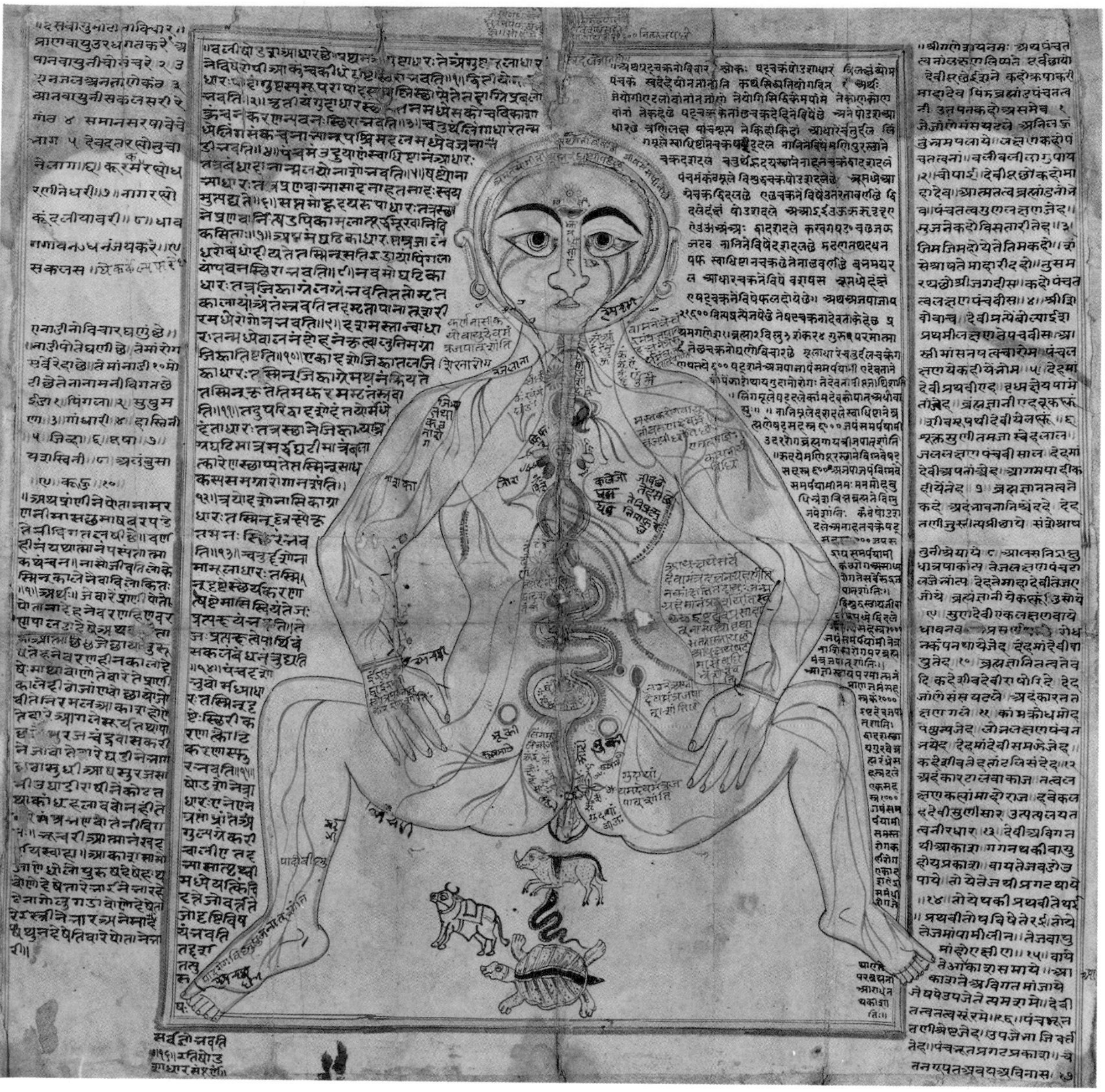

The nāḍīs, the subtle channels of the human body: above left, a diagram from Rajasthan, c. 18th century, ink and colour on paper; above, an illuminated page from Kashmir, c. 18th century, ink and colour on paper. The chief energy channels (below left) are those around the spine: Iḍā, Piṅgalā and Sushumṇā, represented in a leaf from Uttar Pradesh, c. 18th century, gouache on paper

These subtle envelopes are related to the gross or physical particles at several psychic points, and these points are interlinked by numerous subtle channel known as nāḍīs (from the Sanskrit root *nād* meaning motion, vibration). Though attempts have been made to identify these subtle channels with the anatomy of the physical body, they are practically untraceable by direct empirical observation. If the nāḍīs were to be revealed to the eye, the body would appear as a highly complex network.

The most important of the nāḍīs are the central channel, Sushumṇā, and its two flanking channels: the white, 'lunar' nāḍī, Iḍā, on the left, and the red, 'solar' nāḍī, Piṅgalā, on the right. The Sushumṇā nāḍī runs from just below Mūlādhāra, extending to the forehead through the spinal column. Within the Sushumṇā nāḍī there are three more subtle channels: Vajrā, Chitriṇī, and Brahmāṇī or Brahma-nāḍī, the innermost, through which Kuṇḍalinī moves upwards. Two currents of psychic energy flow through Iḍā and Piṅgalā from the perineum at the base of the spine, spiralling in opposite directions around the Sushumṇā, which meets them between the eyebrows. Sushumṇā remains closed at its lower end as long as Kuṇḍalinī is not awakened.

The Kuṇḍalinī energy, Deccan, c. 18th century, gouache on paper

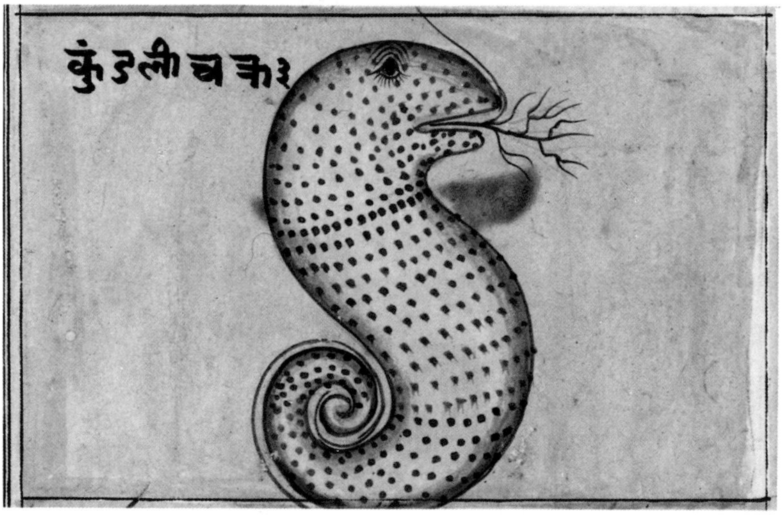

Nāga-bandha – the serpent power in its coiled up, dormant state. Rajasthan, 19th century, ink on paper

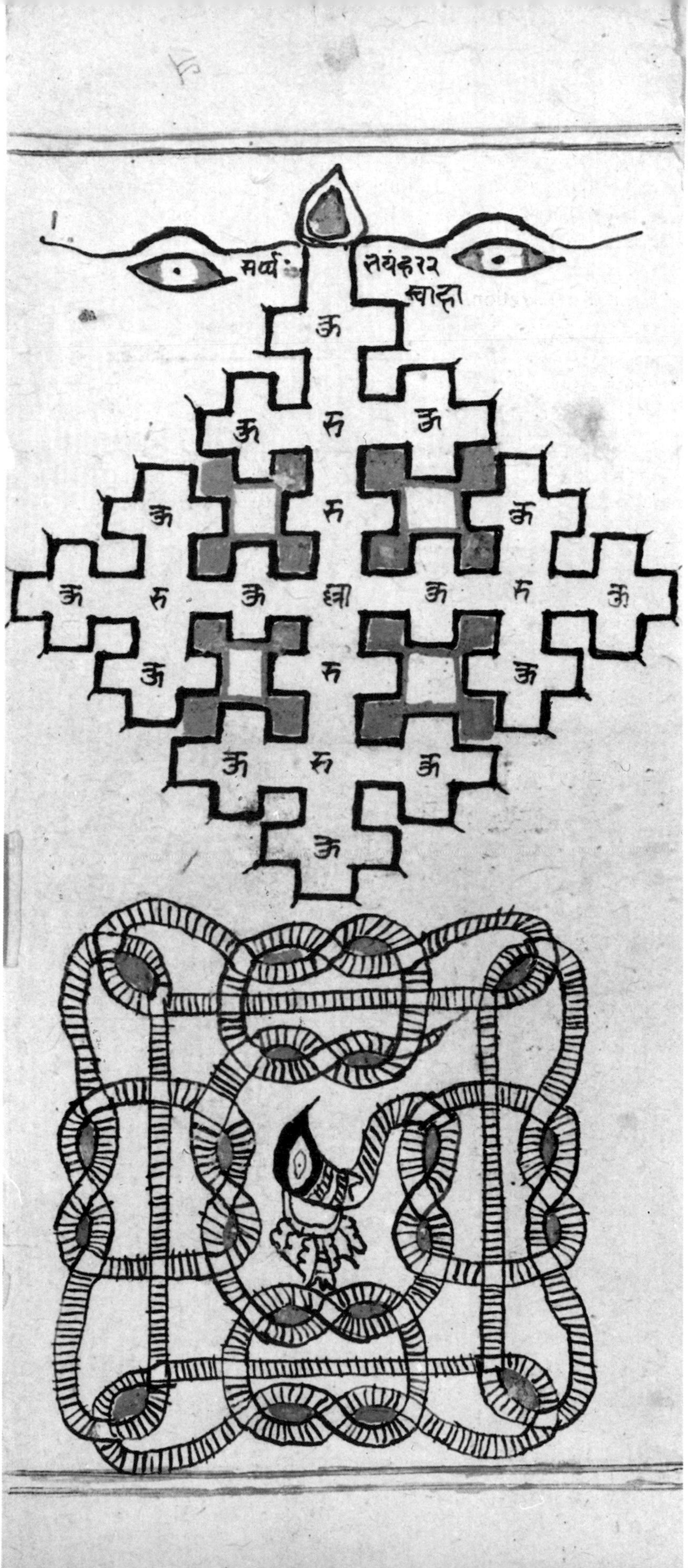

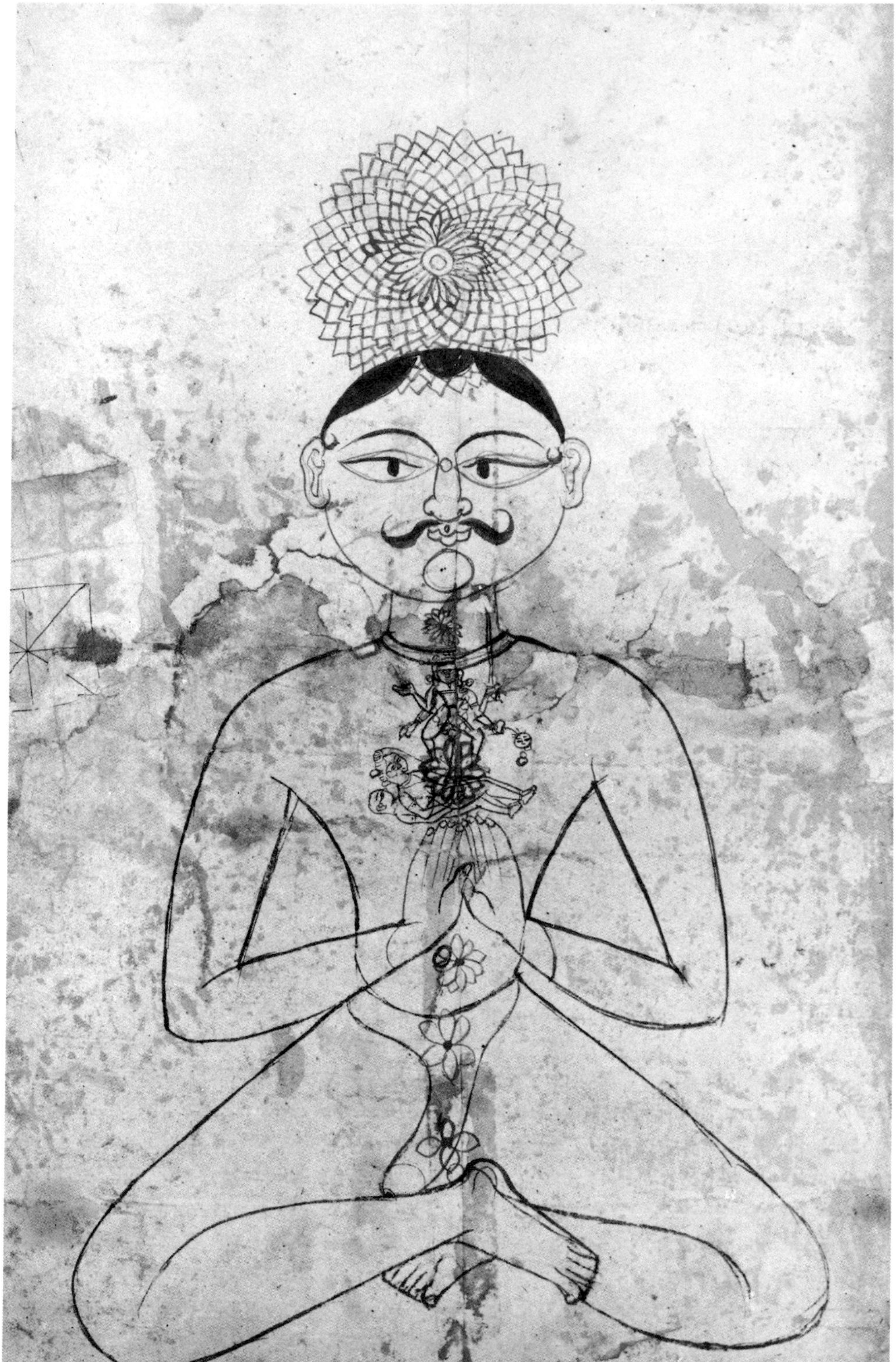

2
The Arousal of Kuṇḍalinī

Long training and preparatory disciplines are undertaken for the arousal of Kuṇḍalinī, but there is no fixed rule, and practices vary considerably. To activate the Kuṇḍalinī energy through yogic methods for the upward journey along the Brahma-nāḍī, the aspirant must summon all the strength and skill at his command. Taking up the posture he finds most suitable, the aspirant initiates the process by which Kuṇḍalinī is aroused through 'sense withdrawal' or pratyāhāra, concentrating all his attention on a single point (dhāraṇā) until normal mental activity is totally suspended. The will-power is directed inwards to the vital air (Prāṇa) that is inhaled and held in Prāṇāyāma, guiding its circulatory movement through Iḍā and Piṅgalā down to the base of the spine into the space where Kuṇḍalinī lies coiled. The entry of Prāṇa produces an abrupt effect like sudden combustion in a confined space, and its heat and sound combine to awake the serpent-power from its trance-sleep (yoga-nidrā). This discipline of psychosomatic regulation and breath-control is the contribution of kuṇḍalinī-yoga to tantric ritual. Prāṇāyāma reinforces the power of meditative practices, and it is upon this technique that the Tantras lay the strongest emphasis.

Breath provides the means of symbiosis between different forms of life and also between existence and awareness. Yoga is concerned to direct this bio-motor force towards the expansion of consciousness in the human organism. It is through the science of breathing that the body's subtle centres are vitalized.

Yoga has developed systematic techniques of breathing, regulating its speed, depth and rhythm. In normal circumstances our breathing is very irregular. Not only are inhalation and exhalation shallow but they lack harmony. While every individual's respiratory cycle reacts dynamically upon the latent Kuṇḍalinī – a reaction that takes place about 21,600 times a day, that is, at a frequency more or less equal to the individual's number of breaths – this respiration is shallow and rapid, filling the lungs to only a fraction of their capacity, and supplying a current of oxygenated

Yogi with the thousand-petalled lotus Sahasrāra – the place of union of Kuṇḍalinī-energy and Cosmic Consciousness – opening above the crown of the head. Rajasthan, 19th century, ink and colour on paper

energy flowing downwards to strike Kuṇḍalinī that is wholly inadequate to awaken her.

Yogananda in his autobiography, while narrating his guru's explanation that the ancient yogis discovered the secret of the link between cosmic consciousness and breath-mastery, writes that: 'The *Kriyā Yogi* mentally directs his life energy to revolve, upward and downward, around the six spinal centers (medullary, cervical, dorsal, lumbar, sacral, and coccygeal plexuses), which correspond to the twelve astral signs of the zodiac, the symbolic Cosmic Man. One half-minute of revolution of energy around the sensitive spinal cord of man affects subtle progress in his evolution; that half-minute of *Kriyā* equals one year of natural spiritual unfoldment.'[2]

Prāṇāyāma is reinforced by such yogic practices as āsanas (sustained postures), mudrās (gestures), mantras (seed-sound syllables) and bandhas (internal 'lock' or muscular contraction). A compact and relaxed bodily position that may be sustained for long periods is first adopted. In Padmāsana, the lotus posture, one sits cross-legged with the right foot resting on the left thigh and the left foot crossed over the right leg; in Siddhāsana, the posture of accomplishment, the left heel is pressed firmly on the perineum and the heel of the right foot is placed on the left thigh, touching the abdomen. In both these positions, the body is upright, with the head, neck and spinal column balanced naturally on their axis. The eyes are directed towards the tip of the nose for deep concentration, while the hands are laid on the knees. Yogis explain that sitting cross-legged

Yoni āsana

Padmāsana

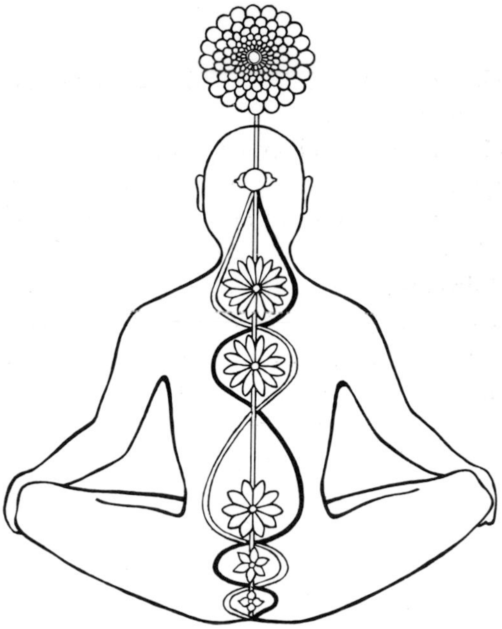

The number of petals in each of the representations of the chakras indicates their respective vibration-frequencies

in either of these postures provides a stable triangular base which sustains the 'closed circuit' of the energy field.

The first step in Prāṇāyāma is to regulate the breathing. Rhythm is all-important, as it is this that supports concentration and harnesses the impulse of the autonomic nervous system. By taking deeper and fuller breaths we begin to absorb the maximum Prāṇic current with each inhalation. To proceed further, a knowledge of the phasing of respiration's units is required. Each unit consists of three parts: inhalation; retention of breath at any point during inhalation, the chief method of absorbing energy from the atmosphere; and exhalation of the used air. Balanced rhythm in breathing depends on achieving the correct ratio between these three units. The ideal phasing of inhalation (pūraka), retention (kumbhaka) and exhalation (rechaka) is 1:4:2.

The air is inhaled slowly through the left nostril (which is connected with the lunar channel, Iḍā) while the right nostril is closed with the thumb. The breath is then held, while meditating on the seed-sound syllable Yaṃ, and exhaled in the correct rhythm. The same procedure is repeated using the right nostril (which is connected with the solar channel, Piṅgalā) and the seed-sound syllable Raṃ. Iḍā and Piṅgalā, as they rise from the region of the coccyx, entwine around the Sushumṇā, crossing from side to side at nodes between the chakras. (It is interesting to note that the same spiral pattern is seen in the double-helix configuration of the DNA-molecule containing the genetic code of life.) In the practice of Prāṇāyāma, these pathways are purified (cleansing of the nāḍīs) to allow the free flow of psychic forces.

The double-helix configuration of the DNA-molecule containing the genetic code of life

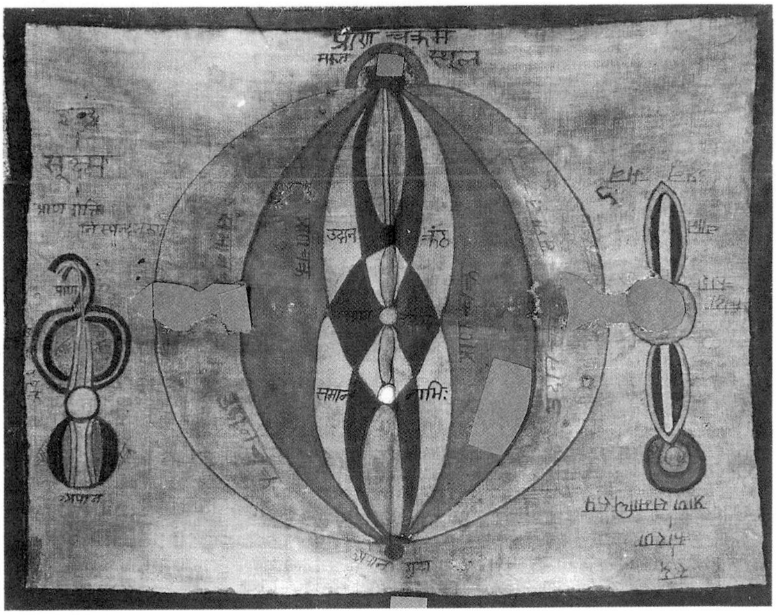

Prāṇāyāma chakra illustrating the circulation of the vital airs Udāna, Prāṇa, Samāna, Apāna and Vyāna. Rajasthan, c. 19th century, gouache on cloth

Prāṇas and the corresponding locations in the human body. From the top, left: Udāna, Prāṇa, Samāna, Apāna; the breath Vyāna involves the whole of the human organism

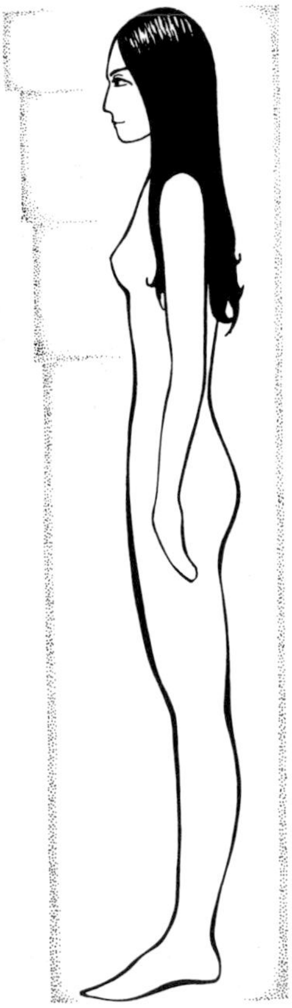

During this yogic discipline, the primal sound Oṃ (A-U-M), or a similar seed-sound syllable drawn from the Sanskrit alphabet, is uttered repeatedly, not only as a measure of duration, but to provide a sound-vibration which has a connection with the subtle channels and chakras; for each chakra has a corresponding sound and colour, vibrating at different frequencies. Starting with the root chakra and working up to the top of the head, these vibration-rates are given by the Tantric texts as 4, 6, 10, 12, 16, 2, 1,000; and the number of 'rays' of tattvas (subtle elements) has been mentioned as 56 for Mūlādhāra, 62 for Svādhisthāna, 52 for Maṇipūra, 54 for Anāhata, 72 for Viśuddha and 64 for Ājñā.

One of the vital airs of Prāṇa is the Apāna, which controls the situation it occupies below the navel region. It is associated with the colours purple and orange, and is linked from below with the fire element. According to the *Yoga Kuṇḍalinī Upanishad* (42–46), 'When one causes the downward Apāna to move upwards [by constriction of the sphincter muscles of the rectum], it is known as Mūlabandha. When the Apāna, moving upwards, reaches the region of the fire [element], the flame of fire, caused by the vital air [Prāṇa] to ascend, increases its intensity. When the fire and Apāna reach the heated Prāṇa, a current is generated in the body. By that current the sleeping Kuṇḍalinī, being very much heated, is roused, and like a snake belaboured with a stick, becomes erect with hissing and by way of entering its hole, reaches the interior of the Brahma-nāḍī.'

Kuṇḍalinī maṇḍala. Nepal, c. 1800, ink and colour on paper

The primal vibration, Oṃ, from which all the elemental sound-forms of mantras emanate. Rajasthan, c. 19th century, ink on paper

I *The chakras of the subtle or etheric body depicted as seven lotuses. Each 'lotus' represents an ascending level of consciousness, as it is pierced and activated by the female energy, Kuṇḍalinī Śakti, Her fusion with the absolute in Sahasrāra is represented in the centre of the chakra by a white footprint (Śiva Consciousness) and a red footprint (Śakti Consciousness). Nepal, c. 17th century, gouache on paper*

II *Scroll depiction of kuṇḍalinī-yoga showing the rising serpent-power dynamized from her slumber. Rajasthan, c. 18th century, ink and gouache on paper*

The cosmic principles moving with the outgoing (i.e. descending) current of vital air are involuted with the starting of the return current. Ascent is to be made in the reverse order to descent. This repeated filling and emptying of breath is the rhythm of the universe itself, sending waves to strike at the root-impulses of Kuṇḍalinī. When Kuṇḍalinī is struck, she awakens, uncoils (i.e. is dynamized), and begins to rise upwards like a fiery serpent, breaking upon each chakra as she ascends, until the Śakti merges with Śiva in laya-yoga (laya = absorption), in deep union, samādhi or enstasis.

It is to the Tantras that we owe the mature development of a system of sound equations (mantra-yoga). Ordinary speech employs sound to express meaning; mantra, the sacral sound, is concerned with sound as being, i.e. with pure sonic vibration. This knowledge did not originate with the Tantras, but with the Vedic *yajña* and the extreme precision necessary to the original science of sacrifice. The Vedantic meditations of the Upanishads continually invoke the mystic *Udgītha* (literally 'ultimate song') of the *praṇava*: Oṃ.

I

द्वितीयंस्वाधिष्ठानचक्रे लिंगस्थाने पीतवर्णो
रजोगुणे प्रकारस्तल देवता सवित्रीशक्ति
वर्णाधिषः कामा णिः उज्जयिनीधार
णास्तलदेवी जाय दवस्था वेखरीवाचा
ऋग्वेद आचार्यलिंग ताभूमिका साधुज्य
ता सेनघटहंसवा हनघट्टहल ९घट
माजा बेंभेमेयेंयें ले यंतमीजा ९
बर्हिःसी जा ८ का
मा १ कामाबा २
तेजसी ५ उलाम ४
चेशिला ५ मिथुनीं ५
देवता अजप
जापघट ५ महा
से ८ ... वटिका ५ पले ५ अत्रदे ४
अजपाजाप्प प्रजामा नासिकीसोहंभावे
नघ्रजयेत अत्रगंथा दिसिसर्पयामिनम्

प्रथमसाधारवक्रे गु दास्थाने रक्तवर्णो रा
तोषोदेवता सिद्धि वदिशक्तिः कूर्मी
ऋधिः मघकवा ह नः अपानवायुः ५
मिंकला प्रेकोवम द्रा मूलबेथः चत्र
दले ४ चत्रमीजा ५ बर्हिःमीजां ४
आनेट १ योगा नंद २ विराने
द ३ योगानेट ४ अजपाजाप
घटशते ५ ...
वटि का ९
पले ५ अत्र
दे ४ ए जामा
नासिकी सोहं भावेन
पूज्रयेत अत्रगं यादिसर्पय
मिनमः जम्बुद्वी प १ धादही प २
कोञ्चही प ३ कुश द्वीप ४ शाल्मलि
द्वीप ५ पुक्करद्वीप ६ सहद्वीप ७ ॥

समही पवती छी ७ मसानलपाल
विराट महीतल
आतिमाजा रसातल
उकार वितल
घोष वतला
कूर्म प्रतला
तला
मला

III

IV

With Nandikeśvara, one of the earliest masters of Śaivāgama, all the sounds known through the Sanskrit alphabet are identified as the vocables sprung from the cosmic drum of Śiva, i.e. of creation itself. Sound is the paradigm of creation, and its dissolution is re-absorption into its source. While this directly inspired the Indian science of phonetic and morphological systems under Pānini, the famous grammarian of the third century BC, it even more directly strengthened speculation into *nāda* (sonic vibration) and its relation to *sphota*: awakening, manifestation-revelation of being. So that by the time we arrive at the Tantras themselves, there is already a sophisticated working tradition and notational system that is three to four thousand years old.

This composite wisdom was carefully guarded, and only entrusted to those who had the spiritual authority (adhikāra) to recognize its significance. While some part of this knowledge was transcribed in the tenth century AD, it is essentially oral and esoteric. For these reasons, it is generally acknowledged that the initiate may only receive the mantra appropriate to his need, stance and chosen deity in accord with his spiritual standing, on the judgment of an experienced preceptor.

According to the Tantras, to 'awaken' a mantra is to activate vibration channels and produces certain superconscious feeling-states which aid the disciple in his sādhanā. The very sound of a mantra, or combination of mantras, has the capacity to arouse the divine forms or their energies. Each divinity possesses a bīja mantra, a seed-sound syllable, which is its equivalent. Thus the bīja mantra Huṃ is the root vibration or atomized form of sound representing the essential nature of Kuṇḍalinī Śakti who 'encompasses the mantra-sounds' (*Lalitā-sahasranāma, 103*). 'The sādhaka [aspirant] whose mind is purified by the practice of *Yama* and *Niyama* [Prāṇāyāma techniques] and other forms of spiritual discipline, learns from his guru the way to the discovery of the great liberation. By means of concentration on the letter Huṃ [the bīja-mantra] he rouses the Kuṇḍalinī, pierces the centre of the Svayaṁbhu-liṅga, the mouth of which is closed, and is therefore invisible, and by means of air and fire places her within the Brahma-randhra.' (*Ṣaṭchakra-nirūpaṇa*, v. 50)

As to the working of the *mantra śakti* (literally 'energy of the mantra') in the arousal of Kuṇḍalinī, the bija mantra repeated according to the rules of the doctrine serves to centre and support the aspirant's auditory perception by its very continuum. In this way it contracts and intensifies the field of awareness to a single point, under pressure of which Kuṇḍalinī stirs towards awakening. It is important to remember, however, that the mantra is not merely

III *Yogi practising nyāsa, placing the fingers on the various sensory-awareness zones of the body with a mantra, so that with the mantra's resonance divine power is gradually projected into the body. Rajasthan, 1858, gouache on paper*

IV *Kuṇḍalinī with Śakti in the fire altar, symbolizing the element fire associated with Maṇipūra chakra whose presiding Śakti is Lākinī. Rajasthan, c. 19th century, gouache on paper*

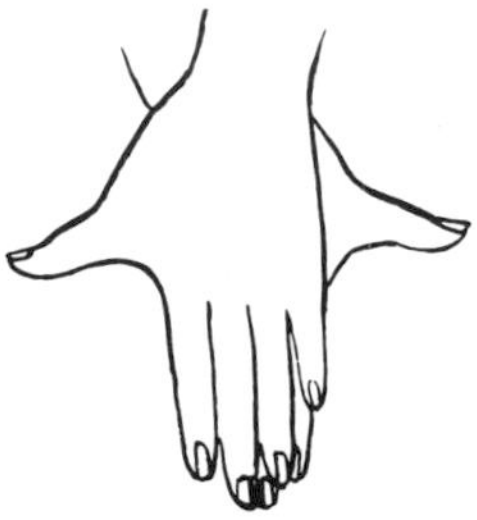

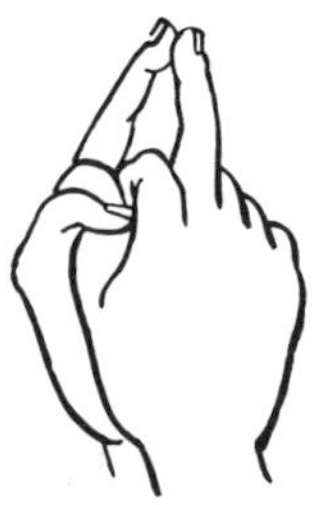

a technique of awakening; it is actually and in itself *a state of being* indicative of the presence of divinity.

As the American researcher Bernbaum writes: 'The mantra bestows no magic power from the outside; rather it releases latent forces within each person which are normally suppressed by the ego. Proper use of the mantra enables the adept to control and direct these forces, primarily toward dissolving the ego and opening himself to the universe within and around him. This control is crucial and is the reason for much of the secrecy around Tantric yoga.'[3]

Kuṇḍalinī is the origin of primordial sound, hence Mūlādhāra chakra has been called 'the birthplace of all sounds'. There are four states of sound: from gross to most subtle, these are Vaikharī (sound manifested as form), Madhyamā (sound in its subtle form), Pashyantī (sound in which the view of the universe is undifferentiated form) and Parā (unmanifest sound). Vaikharī is the level of audible sound produced by the striking together of two surfaces, or the plucking of a string. Madhyamā (from the Sanskrit word for 'medium') is the transition stage between heard sound and inner vibration. With Pashyantī, the sound is heard only by the spiritually-awakened aspirant; and by the time the Parā stage (from the Sanskrit word for 'transcendental' or 'beyond') is reached, sound has passed far beyond the audible. Parā lies deeper than ordinary silence; it is an inner decibel that is experienced as the unrealized root-sound, or sound-potential. It is sound with practically no vibration, which has an infinite wave-length. It is Parā which corresponds to Kuṇḍalinī Śakti.

In accordance with the theory of the four states of sound, it is then shown 'how the fourteen [Sanskrit] vowels [or rather the *a* as their common root] gradually emerge from their latent condition by proceeding, with the Kuṇḍalinī Śakti, from the Mūlādhāra to the navel, the heart, and finally the throat [centres] where the first uttered sound arising is the aspirate, for which reason the Visarga [ḥ] is interpreted literally as 'creation' [sṛṣṭi], its counterpart, the Anusvāra or Bindu being in an analogous way declared to represent the 'withdrawal' [saṃhāra] of speech. The Anusvāra [or Bindu] is also called 'sun' [sūrya], and the Visarga 'moon' [soma], and the sounds *a, i, u, r, l, e, o,* and *ā, ī, ū, ṝ, ḹ, ai, au* are respectively 'sunbeams' and 'moonbeams' and as such connected with day and night and with the nāḍīs called Piṅgalā and Iḍā.'[4]

When Kuṇḍalinī awakens, the aspirant listens to cosmic sound. When the Kuṇḍalinī leaves Mūlādhāra, he hears the chirping of a cricket; when she crosses to Svādhisthāna, the tinkling of an anklet; in the Maṇipūra, the sound of a bell; at the Anāhata, the music of a flute, and finally, when Kuṇḍalinī crosses to Viśuddha, the

cosmic sound Oṃ, the first manifestation of Śiva-Śakti as Sonic Consciousness. The proper knowledge and understanding of Sonic Consciousness leads to the attainment of Supreme Consciousness.

While mantra-śakti acts to awaken and sustain a heightened plane of being-awareness, it has already been prefaced by important, indeed indispensable, supporting means. Nyāsa and mudrā are considered by tantrikas to be the correct way to open the yoga. Nyāsa is the rite by which the aspirant consciously enters the sacred space. It is the cleansing and purifying process in which the body, its key-points and zones of renewal are sensitized by the placing of the fingertips. The body is now 'awakened' from its dormancy and made ready for its sacral role. To the accompaniment of mudrā, it is now offered to the deity. Mudrā is the ritualized body-language both of offering and of surrender. The body is depersonalized and the deity is invited to enter its pure dwelling-place.

Finger-gestures (mudrās), regarded by tantrikas as one of the ways to open the kuṇḍalinī-yoga. Opposite from the top: Mṛiga, Padma, Matsya, Saṃhāra and Gadā mudrās. Above centre: Dhyāna mudrā; below left: Yoni mudrā. Nepal, c. 18th century, ink and colour on paper

Tantrikas believe that the flesh must be 'awakened' from its dormancy. 'This gathering up is effected by cosmicizing the body, and treating it as a 'tool' for inner awareness by taming it with yogic rituals, awakening zones of consciousness and activizing its latent subtle energies.... In the Tantras the relationship of man and cosmos has been reversed, and man himself has 'become' the cosmos. That is, his significance in the cosmic order has been exalted to the extent that he, and his body, are seen as a tool (yantra) of unlimited power, capable of transforming even his baser capacities into eternal values, an exaltation considered as a movement of power from the realm of god to the realm of man.'[5]

Finger-positions (mudrās) are connected with nyāsa in tantric ritual. Ritual gestures create a reaction in the mind of the adept, evoking divine powers in order to intensify concentration. The Yoni-mudrā, for example, represents Śakti's yantra. It is performed with the object of invoking the divinity to infuse the aspirant with her energy. Mudrās such as Vajroli, Aśvani, Sahajoli, Khecharī, and Mahāmudrā are *śakti-chālanās*, 'energy-movers', and are combined with postures, breath-techniques and mantras to awaken Kuṇḍalinī.

The immediate physical world of the body is now pure, impersonal; the mind is poised and alert, the spirit awakened. Having invoked the collaboration of the deity and aroused the coiled energy within, the climb at last begins, and with it the actual drama of tantra-yoga. For unlike the inherited systems of Sāṁkhya-yoga that lead by stillness to the *turīyāvasthā*, the fourth state beyond waking, dreaming and sleeping, kuṇḍalinī-yoga is the dynamic, the kinesthetic way.

Returning to the cosmic axis of the self, the aspirant passes upwards: the graduated planes of unconscious, subconscious and conscious experience open like flowers, yielding under pressure of this charge that mounts from that which is veiled and restricted to a sense of being that is progressively more open, unrestricted, heightened.

The five elements in their increasingly subtle, ascending order: earth, water, fire, air and ether. Combined, they form a progression from outer square to central bindu

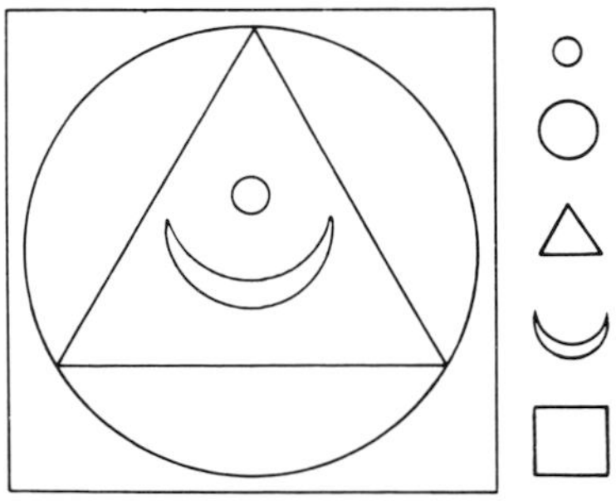

Each knot, each psychic blockage that binds the individual to the common order of knowledge or of action, must be severed in the ascent to truth.

This upward journey through the self refines and subtilizes the energy that is the Kuṇḍalinī, until at the sixth chakra, the Ājñā, centre of command, a qualitative change has taken place. This is, as it were, the last pause in the climb from *sthūla*, concrete and perceptible matter, through *sūkṣma*, the subtle, to *parā*, the causal or ultimate state of being that Kuṇḍalinī will encounter at the *Brahma-randhra*, the 'opening' at the point of perfected being.

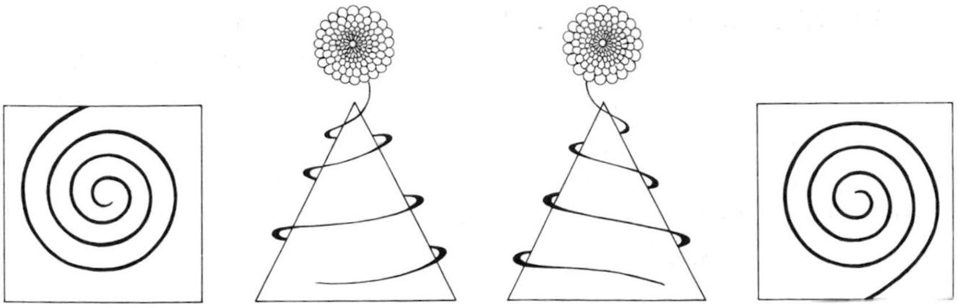

Kuṇḍalinī rising from the root chakra, Mūlādhāra, and having fulfilled herself in the flowering of the Sahasrāra, returning again as the coiled-up energy to sleep in the root chakra

Each of the chakras, according to the Tantras, corresponds to one of the elements of which the known world is compounded, and of which the individual constitution is but a simulacrum. Mūlādhāra represents solidity; Svādhisthāna, liquidity; Maṇipūra, the gaseous; Anāhata, the aerial; Viśuddha, the etheric, or space. One can see the whole process as a progressive transformation of the elements, with an increase of volatility.

In the Viśuddha centre, beyond the four elements, one reaches a sphere of abstraction, the centre of space (ākāśa), the principle of vacuity. There one steps beyond the empirical world; as it were, beyond the 'world of concepts'. C. G. Jung, using the language of archetypes (or the residual images retained in the collective unconscious that surface in dreams, in myths, and in the creative psyche), has suggested the maṇḍala or cone of experience by which to visualize this journey. He sees it as a spiral climb inwards and upwards from the circumference of the sphere or the base of the cone into the point-experience or crest-experience at the centre of being.

A dynamization, transformation and sublimation of the physical, mental, and spiritual state is only possible with the arousal of the Kuṇḍalinī Śakti and her reorientation from downward to upward movement as she rises to unite with Śiva, resulting in the flooding of the whole being with indescribable bliss. The aspirant raises himself from the grosser elements to the subtler, and realizes, in a transcendental experience, his union with Śiva-Śakti, to become a 'cosmic man'.

Details from a meditative series of illustrations depicting Kuṇḍalinī's ascent during kuṇḍalinī-yoga. Rajasthan, c. 18th century, gouache on paper

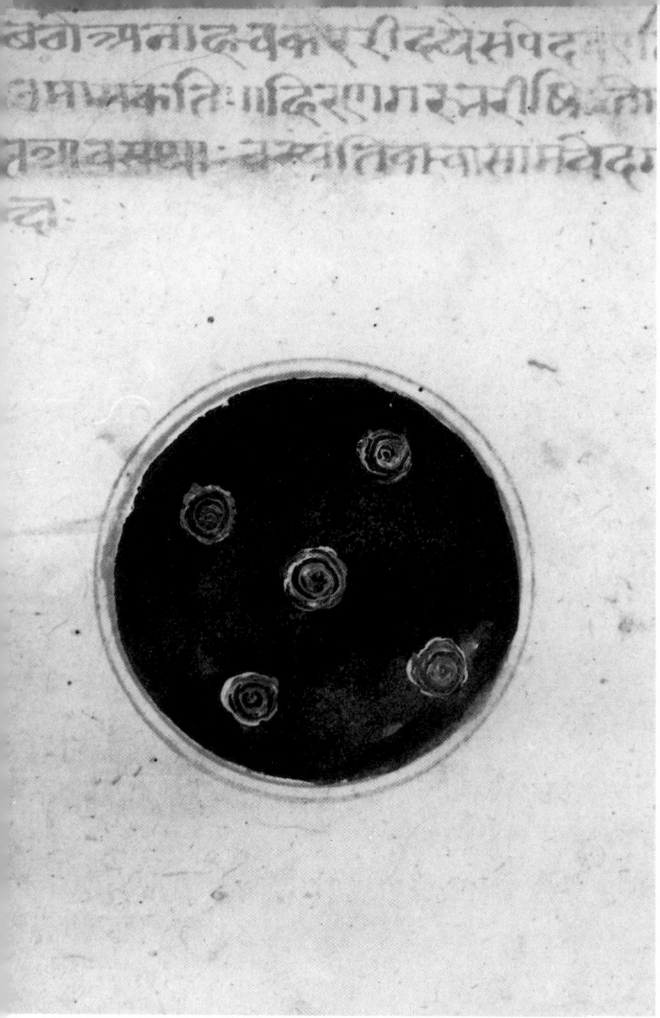

b

a

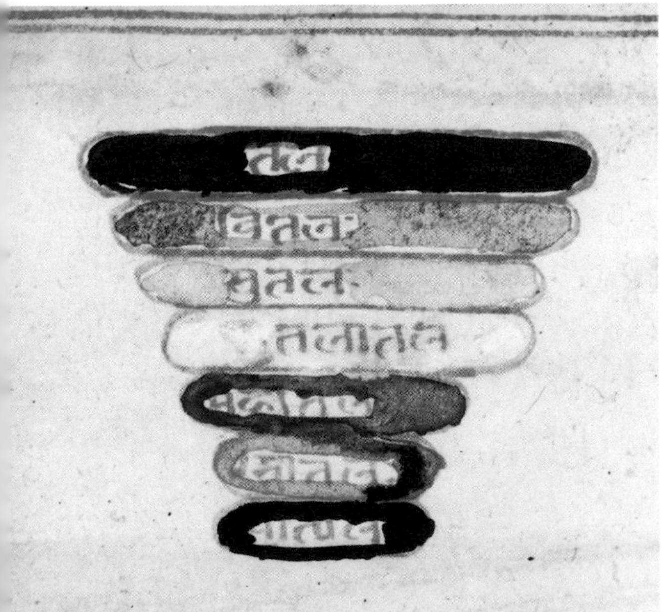

d

c

b

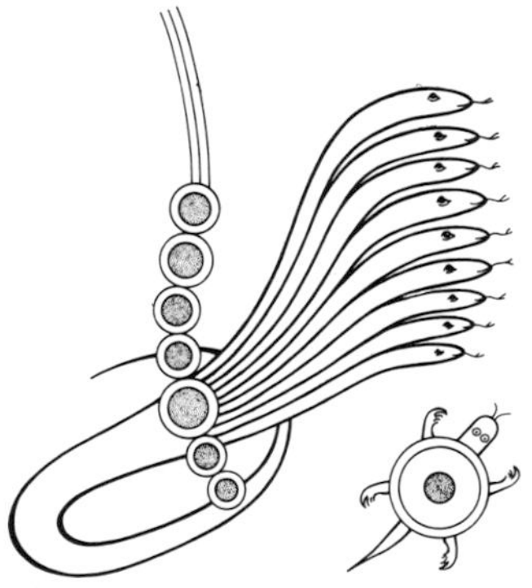

a

Four from a series of abstract meditative images of the chakras, with their corresponding figurative visualizations – as serpent, male deity and female 'energy', and as thousand-petalled lotus. Rajasthan, c. 18th century, gouache on paper

d

c

सातमोविछुद्धकरकंवघान
क्रमरवरण आविदेवता चूसवि
दीयामाकृत विराटवाहनुञु
दीजालधरवाधमिछाकारलादद
तुरीयाचवुमथाफरावरण
वेदजत‌तलिएःसविताःनुवि

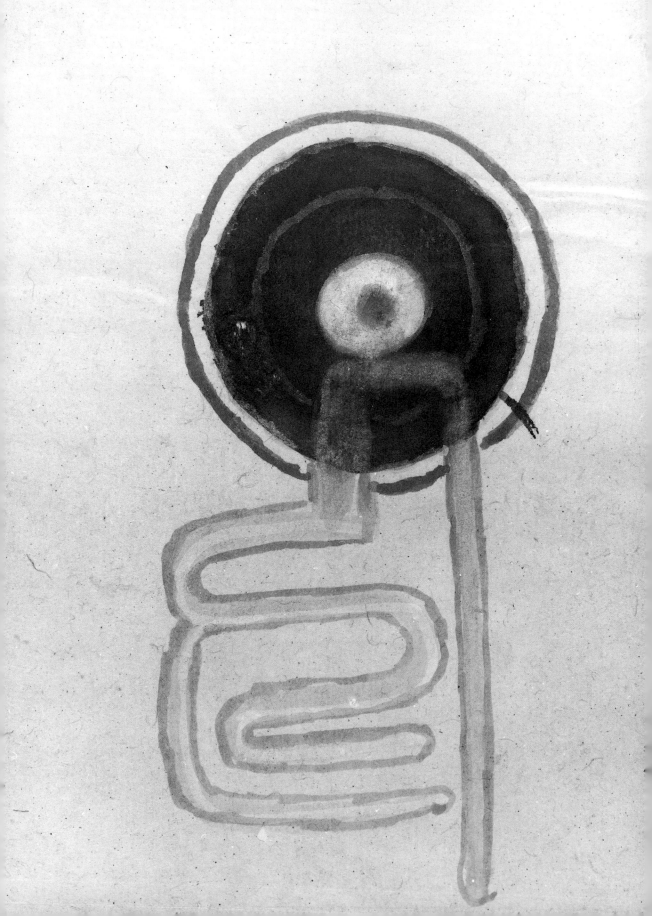

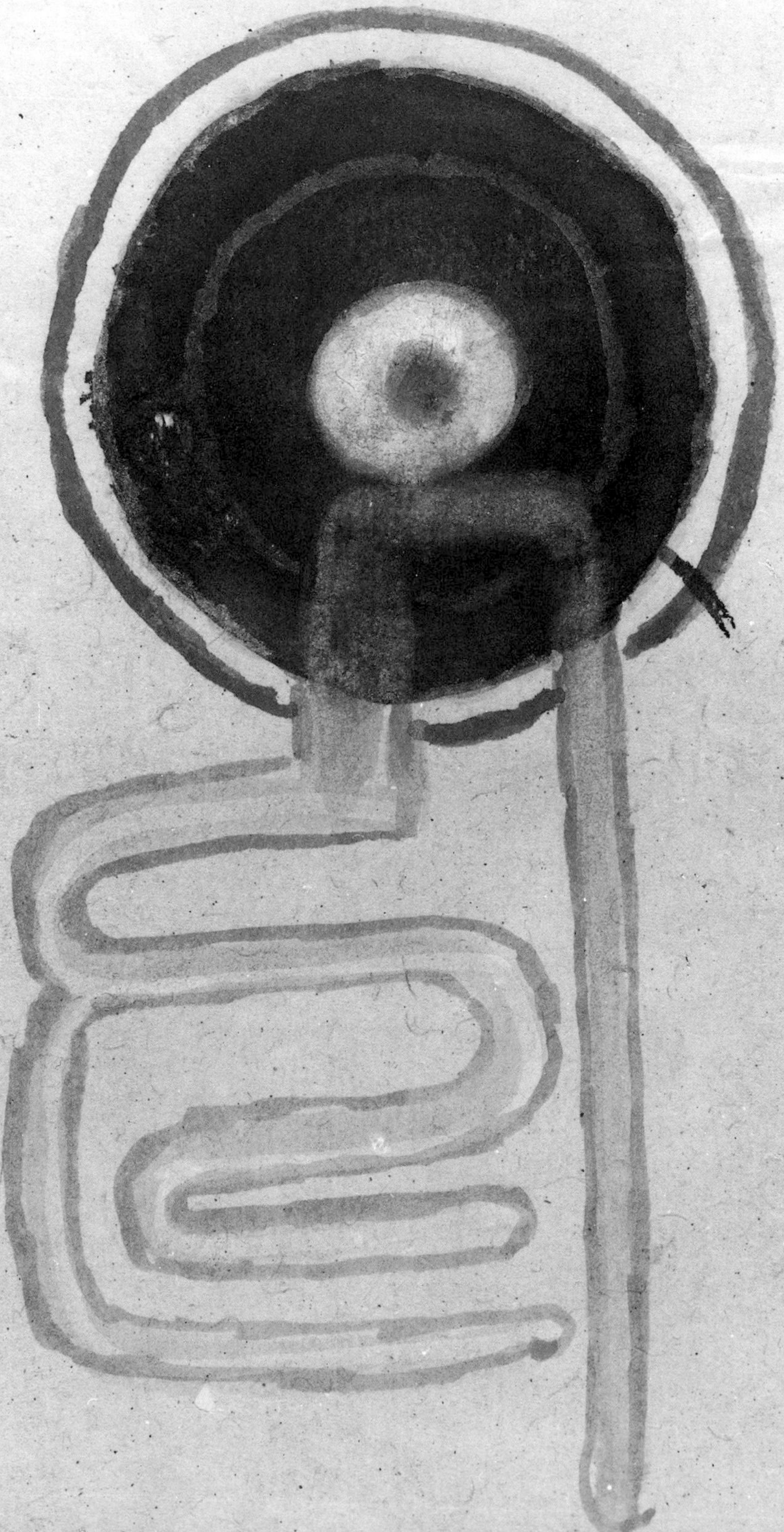

3
Chakras–the Energy Centres

Early scroll paintings often depict the chakras as vortices of energy, without figurative images. However the chakras are more usually represented as lotuses. As Kuṇḍalinī reaches each chakra, that lotus opens and lifts its flower; and as soon as she leaves for a higher chakra, the lotus closes its petals and hangs down, symbolizing the activation of the energies of the chakra and their assimilation to Kuṇḍalinī. The increasing number of lotus petals, in ascending order, may be taken to indicate the rising energy or vibration-frequencies of the respective chakras, each functioning as a 'transformer' of energies from one potency to another.

The Sanskrit letters usually inscribed on the petals indicate sound-vibrations, and also represent the varying intensities of the energies working in the different chakras. Similarly, the colour which each of the chakras reflects is consonant with its vibration-frequency. Each chakra has its appropriate number of petals and corresponding colour: Mūlādhāra is represented as a red lotus of four petals; Svādhisthāna as a vermilion lotus of six petals; Maṇipūra as a blue lotus of ten petals; Anāhata as a lotus of twelve petals of deep red colour; Viśuddha as a lotus of sixteen petals of smoky purple; Ājñā as a lotus of two white petals; and, lastly, Sahasrāra is the thousand-petalled lotus of the light of a thousand suns.

1 Mūlādhāra, the root centre of physical experience at the base of the spine, the sacral plexus, carries on each of its four red petals a letter of the Sanskrit alphabet inscribed in shining yellow or gold: va, śa, ṣa, sa. These letters are contained within a yellow square representing the earth element, together with the seed mantra Laṃ. The four letters represent the root vibration, and are related to the vital breath known as Apāna. An inverted triangle in the centre of the square encloses the unmanifest Kuṇḍalinī in three and a half coils around the black or red svayaṁbhu-liṅga. In the pericarp is found the presiding deity Brahmā in deep red, four-faced, three-eyed, four-armed, holding a trident, a libation jar, a rosary, and in

The cosmic form of Kuṇḍalinī as an energy vortex with the mantra Hṛim. Rajasthan, c. 19th century, gouache on paper

Abhaya mudrā, the gesture of dispelling fear. The deity is the lord of the gross physical or material world. His energy or śakti is called Ḍākinī, and is in shining pink with four arms holding a skulled staff, a trident, a sword and a drinking vessel. This chakra is associated with the qualities of resistance and solidity representing the earth element. The massive elephant with a black strip round its neck is its symbol. The principle (tanmātra) of smell is experienced at this centre.

2 Svādhisthāna, the centre of whatever constitutes the individual's personality, situated in the spine in the region above the genitals, carries on its six vermilion petals the six Sanskrit letters ba, bha, ma, ya, ra, la. In the pericarp, the water element is represented by a half-moon with the seed mantra Vaṃ. Above the mantra is seated the presiding deity Vishṇu in shining dark-blue, four-armed, three-eyed, holding a conch, a mace, a wheel and a lotus. The deity is the all-pervading life-force in the universe. His energy is Rākinī or Chākinī Śakti, in dark blue, three-eyed, four-armed, holding a trident, a lotus, a drum and a chisel, seated on a red lotus. The chakra's associated animal is the light grey or green makara (a sea-monster similar to the crocodile), an emblem of the waters and the vehicle of the god Varuna, lord of the sea. The chakra governs the principle of taste, and the vital breath Prāṇa.

3 Maṇipūra, the 'gem-centre' at the level of the solar plexus, has on its ten blue petals the ten letters ḍa, ḍha, na, ta, tha, da, dha, na, pa, pha. In the centre of the lotus an inverted red triangle, 'radiant like the rising sun', is related to the element fire. The seed mantra is Raṃ. The presiding deity of this chakra is Rudra, who is red in colour, four-armed, holding fire, a rosary, and with the gestures (mudrā) of Vara and Abhaya, granting boons and dispelling fear, seated on the bull. The deity represents the world of mind. The energy generated by him is Lākinī Śakti, in dark blue, three-faced, three-eyed in each face, four-armed, holding fire, vajra (thunderbolt), and making the gestures of granting boons and dispelling fear. Patañjali in his *Yoga Sūtras* (III, 29) says that contemplation of this chakra leads to knowledge of the physical organism and its functions, because this is the chakra of the life-force. The chakra is related to the principle of sight, and also to light, the upward expansiveness of the fiery quality. Its associated animal is the grey or brick-red ram, vehicle of the fire-god Agni, and its vital breath is Samāna.

4 Anāhata, meaning 'unstruck', located at the spinal centre of the region of the heart, has the twelve letters ka, kha, ga, gha, ṅa, ca,

Maṇipūra chakra at the navel centre

Svādhisthāna chakra, below the navel

Mūlādhāra, the base chakra

ccha, ja, jha, jña, ṭa, ṭha, inscribed on its twelve vermilion or deep-red petals. Its seed mantra is Yaṃ. In the centre is a golden triangle, 'lustrous as ten million flashes of lightning', containing the Bāṇa-liṅga. Above the hexagon is the presiding deity Ishā in shining white or brick-red, three-eyed, two-armed, making the gestures of granting boons and dispelling fear. The deity represents the whole world-system in which the diversities of phenomenal realities of space and time are gradually revealed. His energy is called the Kākinī Śakti, in shining yellow, single-faced, three-eyed, four-armed, holding a noose and a skull, and making the gestures of granting boons and dispelling fear. The chakra is associated with the element air and the principle of touch. Its associated animal is the black antelope or gazelle, symbolizing the lightness of physical substance, vehicle of Vāyu, Vedic god of winds, and its vital breath is Prāṇa.

5 Viśuddha, meaning 'pure', is located at the juncture of the spinal column and medula oblongata behind the throat (laryngeal plexus). Its sixteen smoky-purple petals bear the sixteen vowels a, ā, i, ī, u, ū, ṛ, ṝ, ḷ, ḹ, e, ai, o, au, am, ah. Within its pericarp is a white circle, and a triangle inscribed with the seed mantra Haṃ. The presiding deity is Sadāśiva as Ardhvanārīśvara (his androgynous aspect); the right half of the body is white representing Śiva, and the left half is golden representing Śakti. The deity is five-faced, three-eyed, holding a trident, an axe, a sword, a vajra (thunderbolt), fire, Ananta Serpent, a bell, a goad, and a noose, and is making the gestures of dispelling fear. The energy is Sākinī, in shining white, five-faced, three-eyed, four-armed, holding a noose, a goad, a bow and arrow. The chakra is associated with the element ether (ākāśa) and controls the principle of sound related to the sense of hearing. Its associated animal is the celestial moon-white elephant without a band, Airāvata, with six trunks, vehicle of the Vedic god Indra. The vital breath is Udāna.

6 Ājñā, meaning 'command', situated between the eyebrows, controls the various states of concentration realized through meditation, and commands one's whole personality. Its two white petals bear the letters ha and kṣa. At the centre is an inverted moon-white triangle, and within it the Itara-liṅga with the seed mantra Oṃ. Its deity is Paramaśiva, as in the Sahasrāra; he is represented in this chakra in the form of a bindu, symbolizing the inseparable Śiva-Śakti, the cosmic unity whose self-luminous consciousness is all-pervading, all-transcending and all-unifying. His energy is called Hākinī or Siddhakāli, and is moon-white, six-faced, three-eyed, six-armed, holding a book, a skull, a drum, a rosary, and making the gestures of granting boons and dispelling fear, seated on a

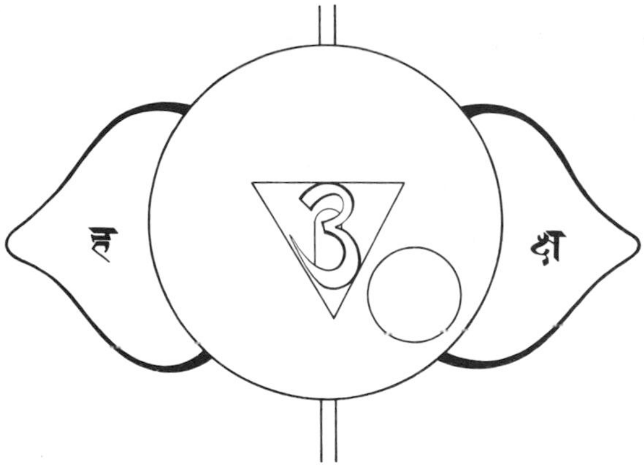

Ājñā chakra between the eyebrows

Viśuddha chakra at the throat centre

Anāhata at the heart centre

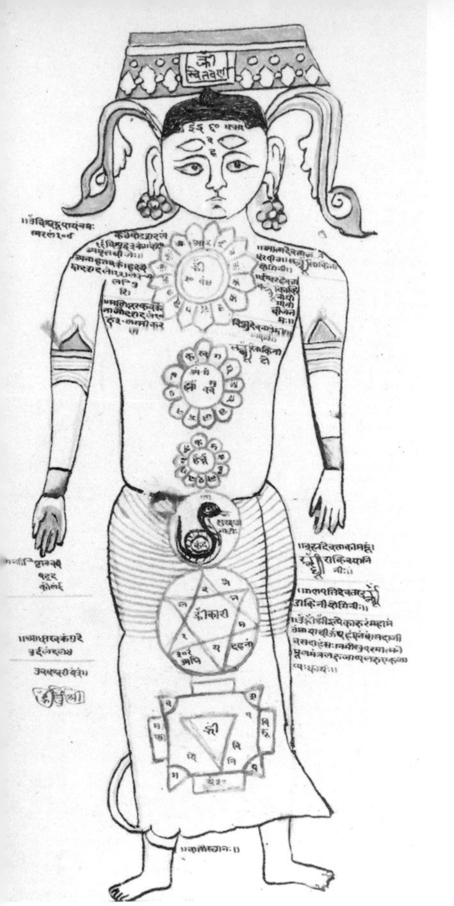

Chakra diagram, Rajasthan, 1900, ink on paper

V *Much is to be learned about the events of the psychic journey of Kuṇḍalinī from the traditional animal-and-deity symbolism of the chakras. The Maṇipūra chakra, located at the level of the solar plexus, is related to sight and to light, to the light-force and the fiery quality. Its animal-symbol is the ram, vehicle of the fire-god Agni. Deccan, c. 1800, gouache on paper*

VI *A Vaishnavite version of Maṇipūra chakra, showing the presiding deity with his Śakti carried on their vehicle, the mythical bird Garuḍa. Deccan, c. 1800, gouache on paper*

white lotus. This chakra is associated with various cognitive faculties of the mind. Both mental images and abstract ideas are experienced at this level. Here for the first time undivided, indivisible existence manifests for the sake of creation as two.

Though Iḍā and Piṅgalā nāḍīs separate from the Sushumṇā channel at the Mūlādhāra chakra, they meet the Sushumṇā in the region of Ājñā chakra, and then again they separate, running into the left and right nostrils.

7 Sahasrāra, meaning 'thousand', is the 'Lotus of the Thousand Petals' located four finger-breadths above the crown of the head. Also called Brahma-randhra, it is the meeting place of Kuṇḍalinī Śakti and Śiva. The petals bear the total sound-potential represented by all the letters of the Sanskrit alphabet, fifty in each layer. The chakra synchronizes all colours, encompasses all senses and all functions, and is all-pervading in its power. The form is the circle transcending various planes in ascending order, and finally, the ultimate state of Mahābindu, the supracosmic and metacosmic transcendental Void. The inverted lotus symbolizes the showering of the subtle body with cosmic radiations. The Sahasrāra is the centre of quintessential consciousness, where integration of all polarities is experienced, and the paradoxical act of transcendence is accomplished in passing beyond ever-changing *saṃsāra* and 'emerging from time and space'.

According to *Gandharvatantra* (Chap. XI), Kuṇḍalinī moving up from Mūlādhāra to Anāhata chakra, shining like molten gold, is known as Fire Kuṇḍalinī; from Anāhata to Viśuddha, as bright as a million suns, as Sun Kuṇḍalinī; from Viśuddha centre to the end of Sushumṇā-nāḍī, lustrous as a million moons, as Moon Kuṇḍalinī. The aspect of Kuṇḍalinī which is beyond Sushumṇā becomes supraconscious, embracing all forms of sound and light.

The essential, however, is not in the complexities of the chakras' symbolism, but rather in their function within the subtle body, the role they play at the moment the Kuṇḍalinī, rising through the Sushumṇā channel toward the top of the head, touches each one on her journey.

The chakras represent a symbolic theory of the psyche. Symbols allow us to see things from the *sūkśma* or subtle aspect. It is as if, through the chakras, we viewed the psyche from the standpoint of a fourth dimension, unlimited by space or time. They represent intuitions about the psyche as a whole, and symbolize the psyche from a cosmic standpoint.

V

VI

VII

VIII

In the terminology of C. G. Jung, in the process of individuation the psyche becomes 'whole' when a balance is achieved between four functions: thinking, feeling, sensing and intuiting. In the system of chakras we find that each phase of energy is represented by an element, in ascending order earth, water, fire, air and ether. Each of the five vortices signifies a new quality, and each is both an extension and a limitation of another. Thus, at the root centre Mūlādhāra associated with the element earth, the 'quality' is cohesiveness and inertia. This level is one in which one may remain content, experiencing no desire to change or to expand into any other state. At the same time, just as the root of a tree implies the possibility of its growth, the earth centre denotes an opportunity to expand the awareness. Likewise the second chakra, Svādisthāna, has the nature of its corresponding element, water: an energy that tends to flow downward. The third chakra, Maṇipūra, associated with the element fire, has an upward, consuming movement like flames. The fourth chakra, Anāhata, associated with air, is characterized by a tendency to revolve in different directions and to relate itself to other possibilities. Here 'air' is not 'vital breath' but the atmosphere, the immensity of space and the conveyor of sound. The name of the chakra implies that it emits a mysterious cosmic vibration, as of unstruck (*anāhata*) sound – that is, sound beyond the realm of the senses. The fifth chakra, Viśuddha, associated with ether, is like a vessel within which all the elements mingle.

The process of becoming is not unilinear – that is, moving in one direction, upward or downward – but is dialectical, with pulls and pushes at every level. The Kuṇḍalinī energy does not shoot up in a straight line, but at each stage of its unfolding unties the knots of different energies. Each successive unlocking brings transformation.

In Tantric teachings (as Jung has pointed out[6]) the Purusha is first seen at the fourth chakra, the heart chakra Anāhata. Purusha is the essence of man, the Supreme Man. In the recognition of feelings and ideas one 'sees' the Purusha. This is the first inkling of a being within one's physical existence that is not 'oneself'; of a being within whom one is contained, greater and more important than oneself but which has a purely psychic existence.

Traditionally, the two interlocking triangles within this chakra symbolize the union of the male principle (the upward-pointing triangle) and the female principle (the downward-pointing triangle), so that here they indicate a cosmic, universal value.

To cross from Anāhata to the fifth chakra Viśuddha, one must admit that all one's psychic 'facts' have nothing to do with material facts. If one has reached this stage, one is beginning to leave Anāhata because one has succeeded in dissolving the 'union of

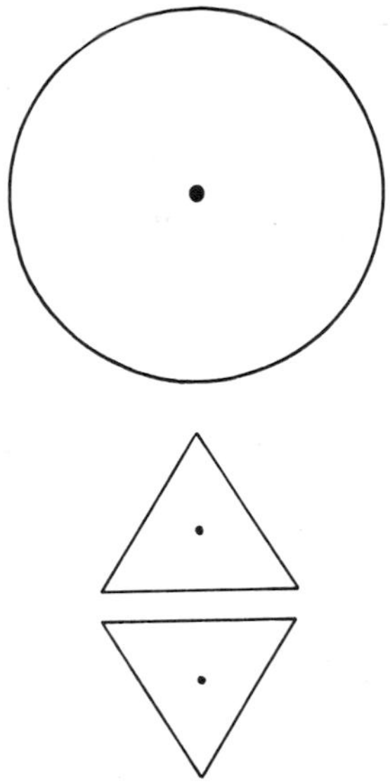

The upward-pointing triangle symbolizing the male principle and the downward-pointing the female principle, and their union represented as a circle with the primal point, the bindu

VII *The chakras represented, not as lotuses, but as abstract energy vortices and as ascending levels of consciousness within the body of Cosmic Man, the Purushakāra Yantra (power-diagram). Rajasthan, c. 18th century, gouache on paper*

VIII *The ascent of Kuṇḍalinī to union. Each chakra is associated with a particular sound-vibration and colour. Nepal, c. 17th century, gouache on paper*

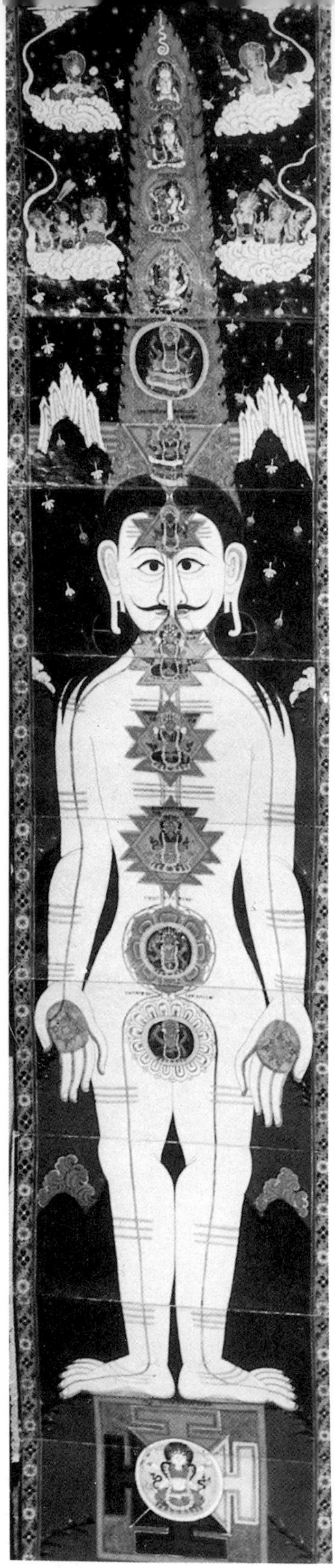

material, external facts with internal or psychic facts'.[7] The element ether related to Viśuddha is the one that is placed 'above the five others' and transcends them.

The presence of the syllable Oṃ within the inner triangle of Ājñā, the sixth chakra, is a clear indication that the associated symbolism is that of the origin, the beginning of all things and also of their end. Oṃ is in equal measure the sonic vibration from which all things emerge, and that into which they must eventually be reabsorbed at the end of the cosmic cycle.

The elements and other symbols associated with the vortices must be understood as referring to the positive and negative polarities functioning within the personality. As Kuṇḍalinī ascends through the planes of the psychic centres, the initiate experiences an interplay of visionary experiences, with sensations of sound, light and colour. At the level of the sixth chakra, Ājñā, the centre between the eyebrows, the dialectical functioning of the personality is controlled by means of a power to command that can harmonize the energies. Just as Jung's subjects in the process of individuation transcend the barriers of polarities interacting within their personalities with the help of a therapist, so in Kuṇḍalinī-yoga the initiate learns through long apprenticeship under the guidance of a guru to balance the dialectical processes of the lower chakras. In Jung's subjects, once a balance is attained, psychic individuation results in an entirely new awareness; so, too, with the adept, when all functions are equilibrated at the level of the Ājñā chakra.

The seventh and last chakra, Sahasrāra, has no associated element, colour or sound. As a lotus, Sahasrāra has a thousand petals, but there is no other specific symbolism connected with it.

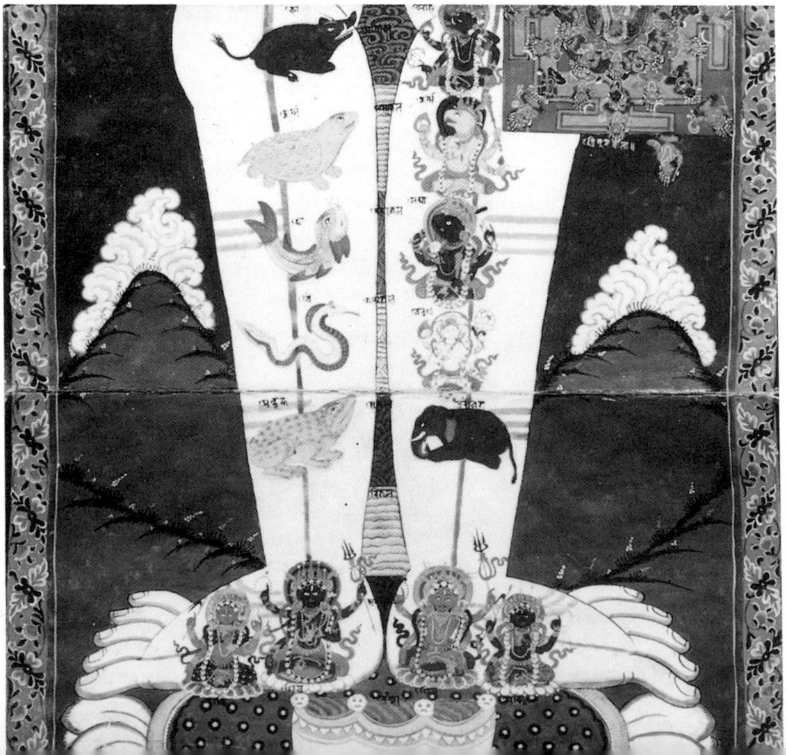

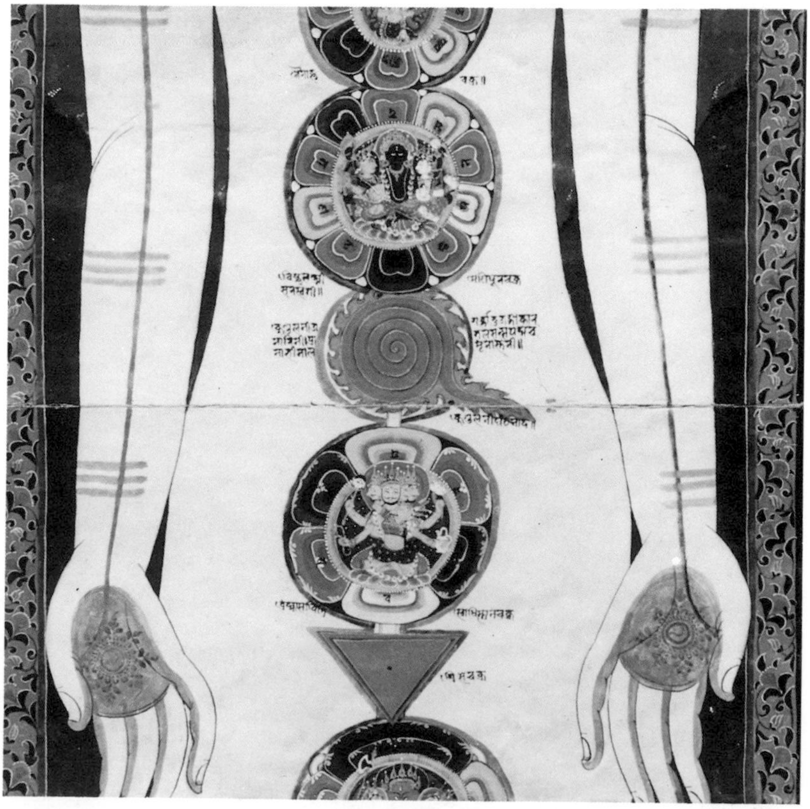

Far left: the cosmic journey complete. Nepal, c. 1860, gouache on paper

The ascent of Kuṇḍalinī commencing at the feet (far left, below) and passing from Mūlādhāra to Maṇipūra chakras (left below), and from Anāhata to Ājñā chakras (left above), each with their related symbols. Details from illuminated manuscript, Nepal, c. 1760, gouache on paper

Oṃ, the primal sound-energy radiating from the ultimate Bindu. Rajasthan, 1900, ink and colour on paper

The colour white, the syllable Oṃ, and the element universal consciousness of the Ājñā chakra admit nothing beyond themselves, unless it be the Absolute, Brahman. To attain Sahasrāra is thus to attain the 'world of Brahman in which liberation is symbolically located. One ought therefore to say that this chakra is located above the crown of the head in order to stress that it is differentiated from the other six. The best graphic representations, indeed, show it in the form of an inverted lotus emitting a radiance that bathes the subtle body in its entirety like the aura.'

Terminating her journey at Sahasrāra, 'the Kuṇḍalinī Śakti, which has the brilliance of lightning and is composed of three guṇas [qualities], after piercing the unmanifest, lustrous abode of Śiva, which is in the form of Bindu [the transcendental centre] and which is situated in the midst of eternal bliss and divine nectar, having the brilliance of a million moons and suns, returns to her resting place, Mūlādhāra.' (*Sāradātilaka*, v. 67)

How long the aspirant will have to stay at each chakra depends on his attachment and karmic action. The root chakra Mūlādhāra, fourth chakra Anāhata and fifth chakra Ājñā are the greatest obstacles to the rising of Kuṇḍalinī. These three chakras are asso-

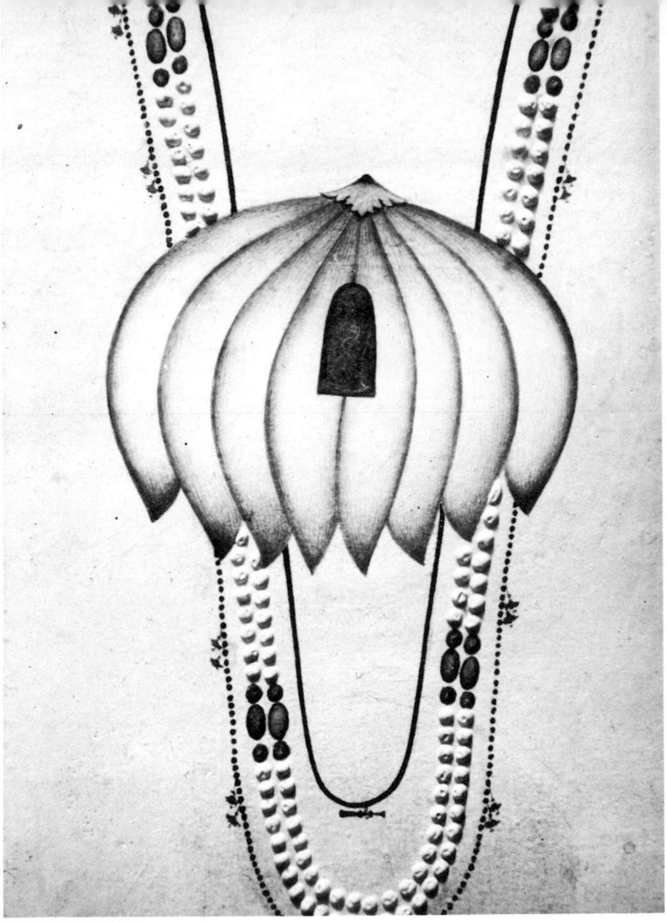

Lotus petals drooping to represent the discharge of energy of each of the psychic centres with the passage of Kuṇḍalinī. The psychic blockage at the level of the heart chakra, Anāhata, is symbolized by the Bāṇa-liṅga represented at the centre of the lotus. Rajasthan, c. 18th century, gouache on paper. Below, a contemporary representation of the Vishṇu knot. Rajasthan, gouache on paper

ciated with the Brahmā, Vishṇu and Rudra knots (granthis), and with psychic blockages called liṅgas (the Svayaṁbhu, Bāṇa and Itara liṅgas respectively). The Sanskrit word liṅgaṃ is derived from the roots, *li*, to dissolve, and *gaṃ*, to go out, which symbolizes 'dissolving and evolving again'. To clear the Brahmā knot is to get established in totality; to clear the Vishṇu knot, to perceive the existence of a universal life-principle; to clear the Rudra knot, to attain the non-dual state, realization of one-ness, the universal joy.

In Jung's analysis[8] of the animal symbols of the chakras, the black elephant at the 'root-supporting' centre of the Mūlādhāra is equated with the tremendous urge that supports human consciousness, the power that forces us to build a conscious world. The element of the Mūlādhāra is, of course, earth, and the force is, at this point, the earth-supporting force.

Jung further observes that when Kuṇḍalinī arrives at the Svādhisthāna chakra it encounters the makara, or Leviathan. As the elephant is to earth, so Leviathan is to the waters: 'It is the power that forces you into consciousness and that sustains you in the conscious world.' Yet its terror, in the Svādhisthāna, lies in its weight and massiveness; it acts to impede progress and must be shaken off.

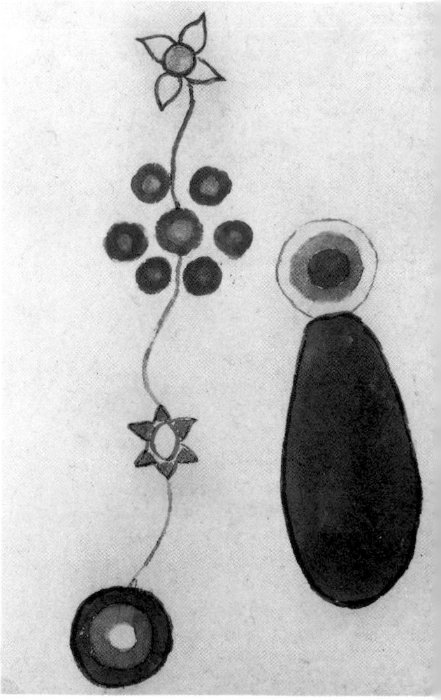

'The greatest blessing in this conscious world is the greatest curse in the unconscious ... so that the makara becomes the dragon that devours you.'

Passing from the Svādhisthāna to the Maṇipūra, from the makara to the ram, we find the animal-energy changes to the sacred beast of Agni, the god of fire: 'The ram, Aries, is the domicilium of Mars; it is the fiery planet of passions, impulsiveness, rashness, violence, and so on.' The ram is a sacrificial animal, though unlike the bull, it is a small sacrifice. 'That is, to sacrifice the passions is not so terribly expensive. The small black animal that is against you is not like the Leviathan of the depths in the chakra before – the danger has already diminished.' To be unconscious of the passions is far worse than to be aware of them as one relinquishes them.

In the transition from Maṇipūra to Anāhata we leave the ram behind for the gazelle, also a sacrificial animal, but with a difference. The gazelle is an exquisite animal, wild and undomesticated. It is shy, elusive, fleet of foot. There is a bird-like quality in the gazelle. It is as light as air, 'gravity-defying', a symbol of 'the lightness of psychical substance: thought and feeling'. The psychic substance, too, is a most elusive thing.

The 'crossing-over' from Maṇipūra to Anāhata, says Jung, is a difficult one, for in it lies the 'recognition' that the 'psyche is self-moving, that it is something genuine which is not yourself, is exceedingly difficult to see and admit. For it means that the consciousness which you call yourself is at an end.' You are no longer master in your own house. It is tantra-yoga, Jung concedes, that recognizes this psychogenic factor as the first recognition of the Purusha, the Cosmic Man.

In the Viśuddha chakra, the elephant reappears, this time as the white Airāvata, bearer of Indra. According to Jung, it represents the insurmountable sacred strength of the animal that now supports the volatile substance of mind. It is the elephant that brought us to birth in the Mūlādhāra. But we can also see that a transubstantiation has taken place. The black is white. The earth is now become ether.

At the Ājñā chakra, the animal symbolism fails and gives way to the liṅga emblem. The corolla of the chakra itself looks like a winged seed. For the ego disappears: 'the psychical is no longer a content in us, we become a content of it'. Instead of the dark germ, the liṅga is 'a full-blazing white light, fully conscious'.

In Ājñā there was still the experience of a self apparently differentiated from the 'object' of God; but in the Sahasrāra chakra, it is not different. 'So the next conclusion would be that there is no object, no God, there is nothing but *brahman*. There is no experience because it is one, it is without a second.'

The Purusha, Cosmic Man. Rajasthan, c. 1700, gouache on cloth

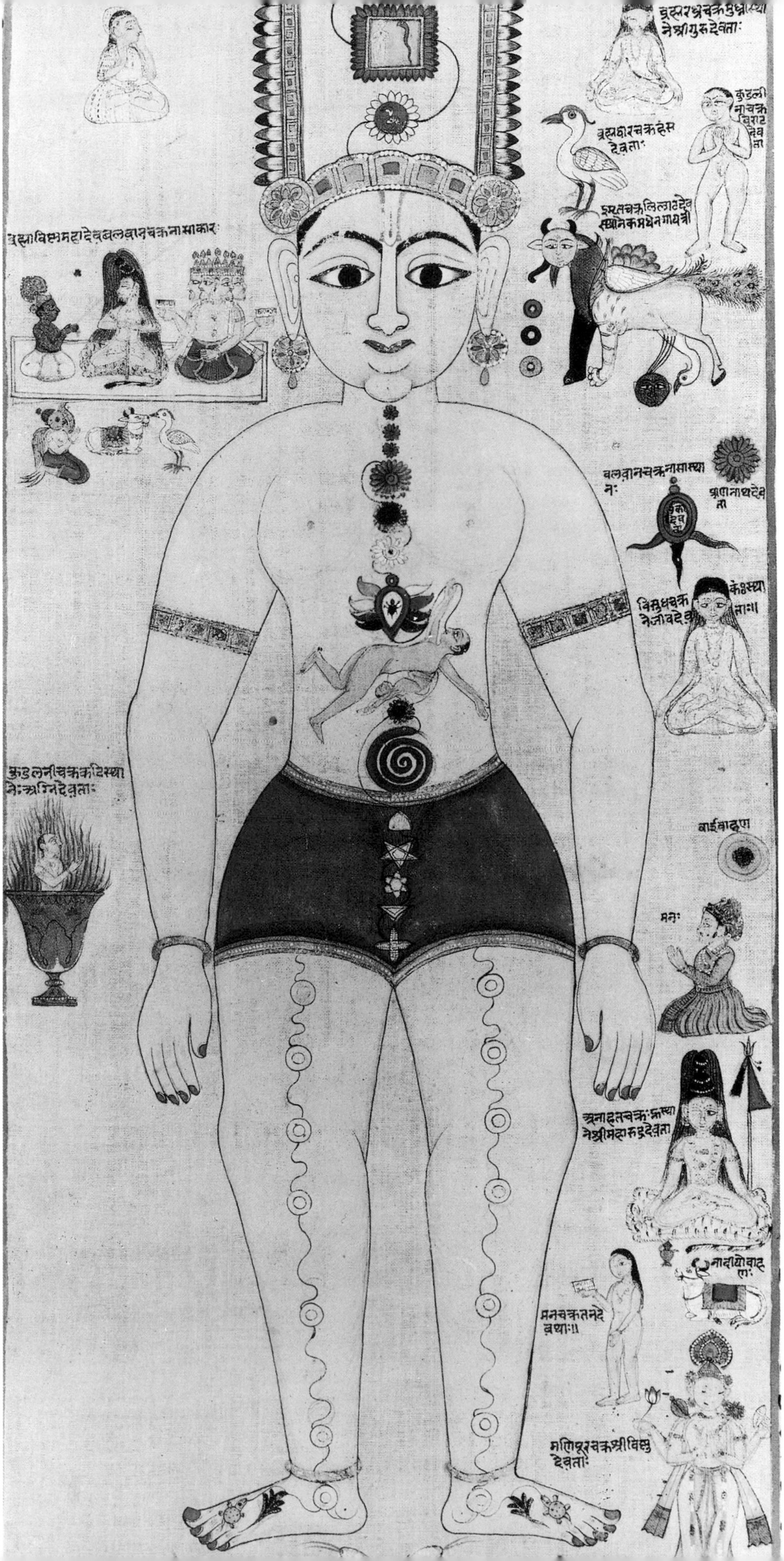

Haridas Chaudhuri gives an account of the integrated functioning of the energy centres: 'Mūlādhāra plays a part in integral knowledge of strengthening the yogi's self-image as a child of the evolving earth-energy. Whereas the libido centre, Svādhisthāna, prevents premature suppression or ascetic annihilation of instinctual drives. It reveals their *raison d'être*, allows their reasonable fulfilment in an organized scheme of living, and then in due time effectuates their transformation into subtle and luminous psychic energy (ojas). The power centre (Maṇipūra) also plays a vital role in integral knowledge as a source of unsuspected abilities for establishing the glory of truth and love in the world. In the Anāhata centre love transforms the joy of being into the joy of giving, the delight of self-existence into the delight of sharing self-expression. The throat centre (Viśuddha), illumined with knowledge and inspired with love, uses the spoken word as an effective tool of communication of the truth of things as they are in their suchness, i.e. in respect of their unique and distinctive feature. The wisdom centre (Ājñā) shines with the light of Cosmic Consciousness and reveals the universe in its unified wholeness of being. But in doing so it does not blot out the infinite richness of multicoloured variations on the cosmic theme. It embraces infinite multiplicity in a flash of intuition and the infinite stream of time in an eternal now. The crown centre (Sahasrāra), functioning in perfect unison with all the lower centres, provides glorious insight into the non-temporal and indefinable depth-dimension of existence. But the integral perspective does not allow this transcendental insight to be fragmented from the holistic and the differentiated aspects of the universe.'[9]

In tantric symbolism the state of samādhi is the union of Śiva and Śakti. If it is true that this total union 'knows no end', it means that the aspirant who has achieved this condition 'will not return', will never again return from his free state as a jīvan-mukta, as 'liberated while yet living'.

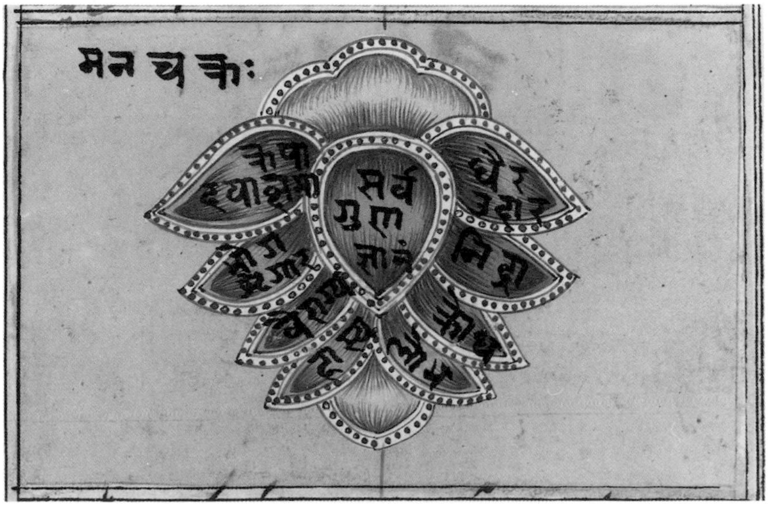

Union of Śiva and Śakti represented in maṇḍala form, for meditation. Nepal, c. 18th century, gouache on paper

Left: Manas (mind) chakra situated above the Ājñā chakra, illustrating the various mental faculties on each petal. Deccan, c. 18th century, gouache on paper

4
Transformation of Energy

In the process of self-realization the highest goal, identified with the arousal of Kuṇḍalinī, is recognized as a microcosmic version of the feminine power of Śakti. The tantrikas identify the power of Śakti with Cosmic Consciousness, since she projects the biunity of male and female principles.

In order to realize this, the discipline of tantra-āsanas (sexo-yogic postures) has developed into a formidable series of psycho-physical practices requiring the same type of discipline as meditation. According to tantra, the Kuṇḍalinī Śakti can be aroused by the practice of tantra-yoga-āsanas, as it asserts: 'One must rise by that by which one may fall.' What on the cosmic plane is fusion of polarities is, on the biological level, the sexual union of āsana – not sexual 'intercourse' as commonly and wrongly stated.

Through the ages, the sex act has been generally associated with procreation or gross physical satisfaction. Tantrikas, however, realized the immense potentiality of sex energy, and, through tantra-āsanas, transformed the energy of sex and freed it to a plane of cosmic awareness. Sex is seen as divine in itself, and a source of a vital energy capable of acting with tremendous force on the physio-psychic state which in turn reacts on the higher cosmic plane.

Tantra prescribes the discipline which sublimates the physical union of man and woman into a creative union of Śiva-Śakti. Among the most important tantric practices undertaken to awaken Kuṇḍalinī are those of Dakshiṇa mārga, the 'right-hand' path, and Vāma marga, the 'left-hand' path. The followers of the left-hand path practise the Pañcha-makāra rites, a term which refers to five ritual ingredients beginning with the letter M: madya, wine, māṁsa, meat, matsya, fish, mudrā, parched cereal, and maithuna, sexual union. The ritual of collective sexual union performed in a circle is known as chakra-pūjā. The fundamental principle of the left-hand path

Latā-sādhanā, a tantric sexo-yogic āsana. Khajuraho, Madhya Pradesh, c. 12th century

Sixty-four Yoginī temple for the performance of chakra-pūjā by left-hand tantrikas. Ranipur-Jharial, Orissa, c. 11th century

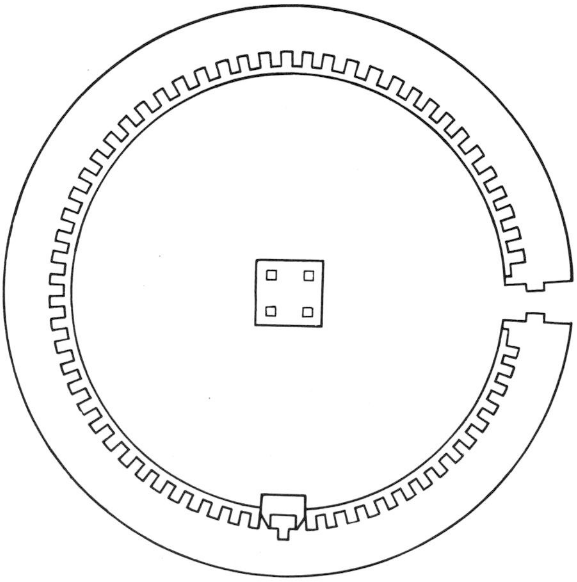

Ground plan of the Sixty-four Yoginī temple. The inner circular wall is partitioned into 64 niches each to accommodate a different female figure of a Yoginī. At the centre of the circle is a square shrine containing an image of Śiva as Bhairava. Ranipur-Jharial, Orissa, c. 11th century

The nude female worshipped at the ritual of tantra-āsana (opposite) is no longer regarded as flesh and blood but as a goddess, as Śakti who embodies the fundamental forces of the cosmos

is that spiritual progress is not to be achieved by shunning or avoiding our desires and passions, but only by transforming those very elements which make us fall, as a means of liberation.

In kuṇḍalinī-yoga the kinetic flow of Kuṇḍalinī Śakti, which in the ordinary course is in a downward direction, is made to reverse to an upward flow, finally to unite it with Śiva, Cosmic Consciousness. To this end, the physiological functions of the body also undergo progressive transformation.

The ritual of tantra-āsana[10] is performed with a partner of the opposite sex. The female participant is seen as the reflection of Śakti, the dynamic female principle of the universe. The 'devout woman' epitomizes the entire nature of the eternal feminine. Prior to the commencement of the ritual, a choice of environment, and determination of propitious time and hour, are made with the help of a guru. It is ideal to have initiation from a Bhairavī (female guru). Tantrikas stress the need to perform rituals in solitary places in an atmosphere free from disturbance and pollution. The acts of bathing, dressing, sitting for worship, offering of flowers and other ritual ingredients, along with rites like nyāsa and bhūta-śudhi (purification of body and elements) are performed to prepare the right atmosphere. The relevant instructions are carried out literally in Vāmāchāra or left-hand practice, but taken in a metaphorical sense in Dakshiṇāchāra or right-hand practice.

In the Pañcha-makāra rite, the nude female worshipped is no longer regarded as flesh and blood but as a goddess, as Śakti who embodies the fundamental forces of the cosmos. 'The transference of divinity is not something which is detached from the real but is within the reach of experience. The man and the woman both are parts of a drama to which they conform in perfect lucidity. Their interplay is a complementary movement of thought and feeling; there is no place for abstraction here, but only constant reference to a tangible human condition. Hence the experience of the transubstantiation of a woman into a goddess is viewed as a very special revelation of reality which can be seen, felt, and apprehended in no other way than what it is.

'The man and woman encounter themselves in one another; in doing so more completely does one relate to one's inner self. This continuous activity of 'seeing' into one another through the various ritual acts climaxing in sexo-yogic-āsana plunges the group into an anonymity in which personal ego-sense is dissolved for the acceptance of the common goal. By the process of ritual projection, the adepts are imbued with divinity until both the male and female, who represent the dialectical principles, achieve an existential awareness of unity similar to the symbol of the circle: "So 'ham:

I am He" or "Sā 'ham: I am She", for "There is no difference between Me and Thee."'[11]

Sexual energy is also tapped through Haṭha-yoga and other processes such as Padmāsana, Siddhāsana, Yoni āsana, Rati āsana, and by means of certain mudrās, the most important being Vajroli, Sahajoli, Yoni, Khecharī, Aśvani and Mahāmudrā. Through bandhas, contraction of the pelvic region is also possible, the most effective being the Uḍḍiyāna and Mūla-bandha.

Eliade writes: 'This is what the Haṭha-yogins do when they unite the 'sun' and 'moon'. The paradoxical act takes place on several planes at once: through the union of Śakti [= Kuṇḍalinī] with Śiva in the Sahasrāra, the yogin brings about inversion of the cosmic process, regression to the indiscriminate state of the original Totality; 'physiologically', the conjunction sun-moon is represented by the 'union' of the Prāṇa and Apāna – that is, by a 'totalization' of the breaths; in short, by their arrest; finally, sexual union, through the action of the vajrolimudrā, realizes the 'return of semen'.'[12] It is claimed that the body's richest blood produces the reproductive ingredients in both sexes, and that, from this, an indefinable power, ojas, is generated in the body. This *élan vital* is stored up during the span of one life, and from this, our micro-macrocosm structure draws its substance.

Vivekananda writes: 'The yogis claim that of all the energies that are in the human body the highest is what they call 'ojas'. Now this ojas is stored up in the brain, and the more ojas is in a man's head the more powerful he is, the more intellectual, the more spiritually strong.'[13] According to Dr Mishra, 'the endocrine secretions that are constantly passing in the blood are utilized in the formation of *ojas śakti.* The essence of hormonal energy is called *ojas* ... There are two *ojas*: *parā ojas*, which supplies the heart – and *aparā ojas*, which circulates constantly through the blood vessels to nourish the entire body, to heal mental and physical diseases.'[14]

Asana is meant for the control of the body and mind, to permit the free flow of psychic forces through the physiological mechanisms. It is a unitive, contemplative way, an altered state, through which a new reality evolves, a new unit comes into existence in which the old two are lost. 'Sexuality and spirituality become two ends of one energy.' As Rajneesh remarks: 'Tantric sexual union is falling in love with the Whole Cosmos, it is a total surrender to the Whole Cosmos.' In surrendering we become feminine, the feminine depths of our psyche then dissolving, transcending – a total experience of oneness – and a tremendous energy is released. From the tantric point of view, the consummated human being is man and woman

Young ascetic Śiva preparing a highly intoxicant drink, 'bhāṅg' made of hemp leaves. Kangra School, c. 1850, gouache on paper

fused into a single unit. When the idea of basic unity, that the two are inseparable, emerges, the state of ānanda, of infinite joy or perpetual bliss, is reached. This state of bliss is the closest approximation one may experience to the state of liberation. The inner life-force is aroused to its full potential through the mystic process of awakening the Kuṇḍalinī Śakti.

'One who has attained transformation, a spiritual rebirth, has no more desires. All external aids become symbols of phases and forces. They are no more than 'links' of different parts of the whole, and all the means that we require to reach the ultimate goal, however high, lie within us. "What need have I of an outer woman? I have an inner woman within myself," as tantra says. When roused, Kuṇḍalinī, the 'inner woman', shines like 'millions of lightning flashes' in the centre of the sādhaka's body. He then thinks that he himself is shining like everything that is reflected. He looks upon the entire objective world that is reflected as surging within him.'[15]

This crucial experience is one of the great moments of our spiritual existence. Both internal and external practices are imperative, because long ago, these revealed to the yogis a truth which has opened up a new understanding of the web of power in which we are living.

Sometimes the use of psychedelic preparations is prescribed to attain the desired result. Swami Satyananda's remarks on this method are pertinent. 'The fourth method of awakening according to Yoga is through herbs. In Sanskrit, the word is Aus̒hadhi, but it should not [be taken to] mean drugs. Through herbs either the partial or the fuller awakening can be brought about; either the awakening of Iḍā or Piṅgalā, or the awakening of Sushumṇā which means the entire, total awakening....That is known as Auśhadhi. But it is also said that the herbs which should be used to awaken this potentiality, or this life-force in man, should be understood or should be got only through the Guru, not without a Guru. Because there are certain herbs that awaken Iḍā and there are others that awaken Piṅgalā only; and there are those that can even suppress both of these two, so that you can go to the mental asylum very quickly! So Auśhadhi or the herbal awakening is a very risky, a quick but unreliable method. It should only be got from one who is a very reliable person, and who knows the science very well.'[16]

The potential exploratory value of substances considered to be charged with prāṇic energies may be very striking, but for the unprepared, their use to attain altered states of consciousness is likely to give rise to many problems.

'In the case of drug-induced states – especially the first few instances – the trip is likely to be highly uncontrolled. The individual will find himself hurled into some far-flung region of inner space, with little chance to absorb or even notice the intervening regions. The drug takes his awareness, as it were, and flings it out to an unfamiliar realm of consciousness. Without adequate preparation, the traveller feels totally disoriented.... Finally, with drugs, the trip is of limited duration. One always comes down, or comes back.'[17]

Peak experiences can occur when there is deep emotional resonance and mutual understanding during sexual intercourse, or during the delivery of a child. Under these circumstances one can transcend individual boundaries, and experience feelings of oneness due to Kuṇḍalinī's split-second arousal. However, even 'if the sexual intercourse and the delivery of a child occur under optimal circumstances and have a cosmic quality, they seem to have a certain degree of inherent ambiguity. During sexual intercourse, the partners can experience glimpses of cosmic unity and transcend their feelings of individual separateness. At the same time, this sexual union can lead to the conception of a new individual and send him or her on the way toward isolation from cosmic consciousness and in the direction of increasing individualization and alienation. Similarly, while the mother is experiencing cosmic feelings during the delivery of her child, the newborn is confronted with the agony of birth and trauma of separation. The emotional and physical pain involved in this process then becomes the decisive factor alienating the new individual from undifferentiated cosmic consciousness that he or she experienced as a fetus.'[18]

IX *Vajra in union with his female Wisdom. In kuṇḍalinī-yoga the flow of Kuṇḍalinī energy, which in the ordinary course is in a downward direction, is made to reverse to an upward flow, finally to unite with Cosmic Consciousness. This state of ultimate bliss (ānanda) is a transcendence of dualities – male-female, energy-consciousness, Śiva-Śakti. Tibet, c. 19th century, gouache on cloth*

X *Śiva-Śakti as Kāmeśvara and Kāmesvari, the androgynous form, half male and half female, indicating that male and female principles and attributes conjoined signify psychic totality. Pahari School, c. 18th century, gouache on paper*

IX

X

XI

नाली मूल त्रयातीत　गुणातीत चैतन्यात्म

सर्वव्यापीसवमात्रा स　वंदल वेराट टेरशि

दल घरावा मोदे　वेद ग्रनपमस्थान

नयाजीण एकसह　सें ꞏꞏ चटिका

दले षट　ग्रदरें रꞏ

सोहंसे　ख्या रꞏ

एकविंश　निसह

णिशट,　शातानि

नयेंवच　निशा हे

वहनिश्राण　सचकाल

विनश्पति स　कारेणबदि

तिहकारेणवसे　ख्नुनः हेसहेसल

कामंत्रंजीवाजनपंतिस　वेद ग्राधारेलिंगना

प्रकटितहृदये नाल　मूलेललाटे होपवेष

डशोरेहिटशदशद　लेहदशार्थेचबके

सानेबालमधेडफ　कफसहितिनेकेवदेशे

नां हेनेतनार्थेयुके　सकलदलगानेवहि

Whereas, 'the journey the meditator takes is one which seems to encompass the same spaces, but the trip is much more gradual and more under the control of the meditator. Because the journey is of necessity slower and more systematic, it appears easier to assimilate the insights which come through meditation. Indeed, over the years this kind of integration seems to occur almost automatically, according to the rate of change of the meditator's nervous system and his psychological development. Since there are no chemicals involved – in fact, systematic meditation seems to result in a lessened tendency to use chemical means of altering awareness – meditation is generally regarded as providing a purer trip.'[19]

As another Western observer has written of the question of drug-use: 'Persons who practice mantra meditation have been found to show evidences of increased integration in their life activities. For example, one study reports that eighty-three per cent of a large group of drug users practising this kind of meditation gave up the use of drugs.'[20]

XI *Tantric āsana, the ritual of union in which the sexual energy is transformed to the spiritual plane through āsana disciplines. Kangra School, c.1850, gouache on paper*

XII *The union of Śiva and Śakti at the Sahasrāra chakra, symbolized by the thousand-petalled lotus. Central to tantra's view is the concept that the ultimate Reality is unity, an indivisible whole. As Cosmic Consciousness – Śiva and his power, Śakti – it cannot be differentiated since it projects the bi-unity of male and female principles. Detail of a scroll painting on kuṇḍalinī-yoga. Rajasthan, c. 18th century, gouache on paper*

Above left: Sahasrāra chakra, detail from a kuṇḍalinī-yoga manuscript. Rajasthan, c.1800, gouache on paper

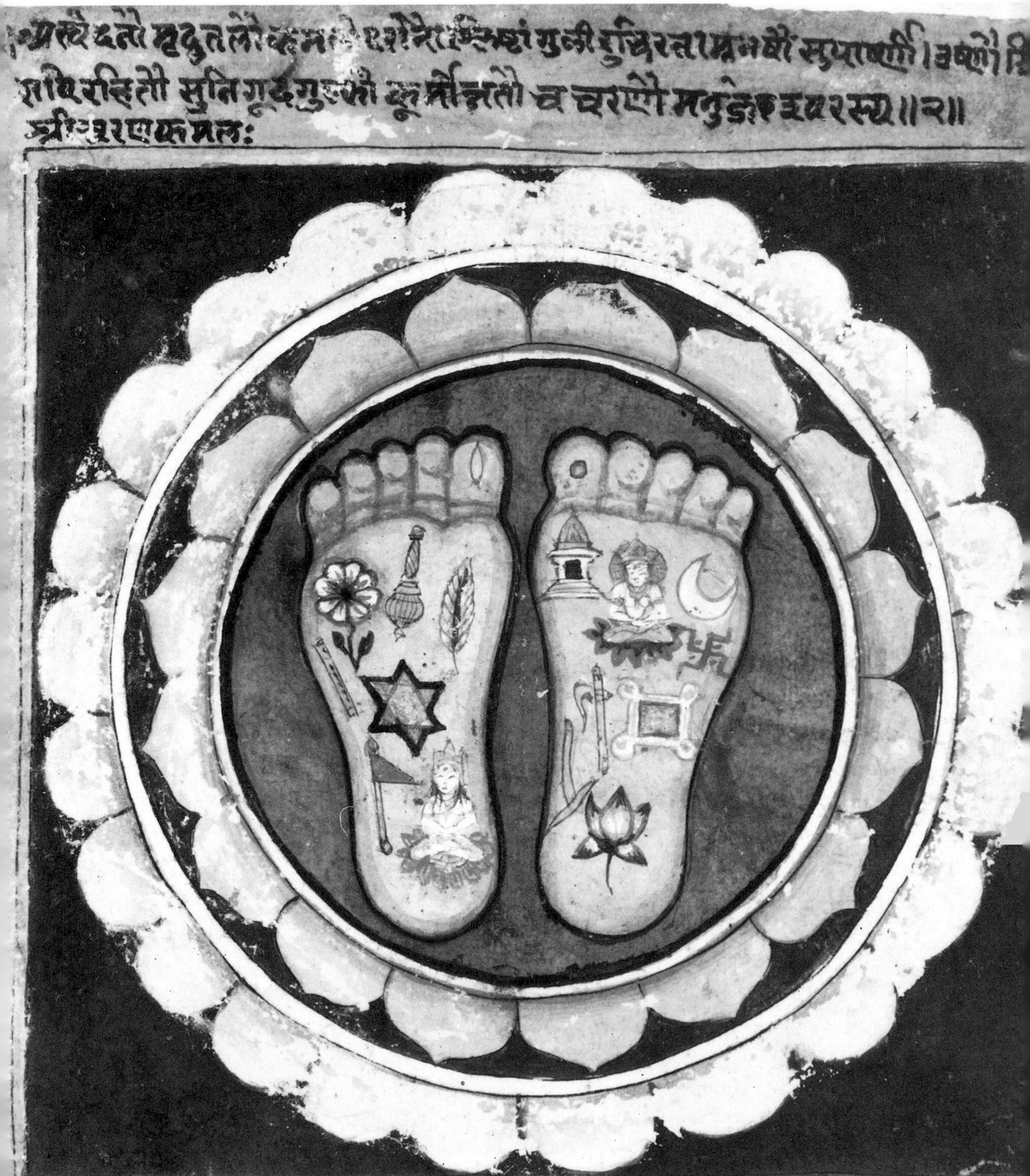
श्रीचरणकमल:

5
The Kuṇḍalinī Experience Classical and Clinical

The ascent of Kuṇḍalinī as it pierces through the chakras is manifested in certain physical and psychic signs. Yogis have described the trembling of the body which precedes the arousal of Kuṇḍalinī, and the explosion of heat which passes like a current through the Sushumṇā. During Kuṇḍalinī's ascent, inner sounds are heard, resembling a waterfall, the humming of bees, the sound of a bell, a flute, the tinkling of ornaments, and so on. The head may start to feel giddy and the mouth fill with saliva, but the yogi goes on until he can hear the innermost, the most subtle, the 'unstruck' sound (anāhata nād). In his closed-eye perception the yogi visualizes a variety of forms, such as dots of light, flames, geometrical shapes, that in the final state of illumination dissolve into an inner radiance of intensely bright, pure light.

Dhyanyogi Madhusudandas, a contemporary guru following the traditional methods of kuṇḍalinī-yoga, enumerates the numerous signs and symptoms that may be experienced by the aspirant as: creeping sensations in the spinal cord; tingling sensations all over the body; heaviness in the head or sometimes giddiness; automatic and involuntary laughing or crying; hearing unusual noises; seeing visions of deities or saints. Dream-scenes of all kinds may appear, from the heavenly to the demonic. Physically, the abdomen wall may become flat and be drawn towards the spine; there may be diarrhoea or constipation; the anus contracts and is drawn up; the chin may press down against the neck; the eyeballs roll upwards or rotate; the body may bend forward or back, or even roll around on the floor; breathing may be constricted, seeming sometimes to cease altogether, although in fact it does not, but merely becomes extremely slight; the mind becomes empty and there is an experience of being a witness in the body. There may be a feeling of Prāṇa flowing in the brain or spinal cord. Sometimes there is a spontaneous chanting of mantras or songs, or simply vocal noises. The eyes may

The feet of Vishṇu. In Hindu esoteric tradition the heel and great toe contain subtle channels second only in importance to the nāḍīs of the spine. Through them the primal energy enters the physical body. Rajasthan, c. 18th century, gouache on paper

not open in spite of one's efforts to open them. The body may revolve or twist in all directions. Sometimes it bounds up and down with crossed legs, or creeps about, snake-like, on the floor. Some perform āsanas (yogic postures) both known and unknown; sometimes the hands move in classic, formal dance-patterns, even though the meditator knows nothing of dance. Some speak in tongues. Sometimes the body feels as if it is floating upwards, and sometimes as if it is being pressed down into the earth. It may feel as if it has grown hugely large, or extremely small. It may shake and tremble and become limp, or turn as rigid as stone. Sometimes the brows knit, and the face wrinkles up tightly, closing the eyes. Some get more appetite, some feel aversion to food. Even when engaged in activities other than meditation, the aspirant who concentrates his mind experiences movements of prāṇa-śakti all over the body, or slight tremors. There may be aches in the body, or a rise or drop in temperature. Some people become lethargic and averse to work. Sometimes the meditator hears buzzing sounds as of blowing conches, or bird-song or ringing bells. Questions may arise in the mind and be spontaneously answered during meditation. Sometimes the tongue sticks to the palate or is drawn back towards the throat, or protrudes from the mouth. Salivation increases or decreases. The throat may get dry or parched. The jaws may become clenched, but after a time they reopen. One may start yawning when one sits for meditation. There may be a feeling of the head becoming separated from the body, and one may experience 'headlessness'. Sometimes one may be able to see things around one even with the eyes closed. Various types of intuitive knowledge may begin. One may see one's own image. One may even see one's own body lying dead. From all these signs, one may know that Kuṇḍalinī Śakti has become active.

Not everyone will experience all or even most of these signs. The Śakti produces whatever experiences are necessary for the disciple's spiritual progress, according to his *saṃskāras*, or habit-pattern formed by past action.

Swami Muktananda, initiated by his spiritual preceptor, describes in his autobiographical account his heaviness of head, his sensations of heat, of pain at the base of the spine, the involuntary movements, flows of energy through the body, unusual breathing-patterns, inner lights and sounds, visions and voices, and many other extraordinary experiences.

In the process of the arousal of Kuṇḍalinī, Muktananda went through an experience of extreme sexual excitement: 'Every day brought new *kriyās* and new experiences. One day, my body and senses became possessed by sexual desire.... I was meditating in my hut at Suki, and in meditation I was seeing the red light. I was happy. Then, in the middle of my meditation, came a *kriyā* that was utterly humiliating.... All the love and intoxication I had felt in meditation left me.... Instead, in their place came a powerful sexual desire.... I could think of nothing but sex! My whole body boiled with lust, and I cannot describe the agony of my sexual organ.... I decided to make my body weaker and thinner, so I stopped drinking milk and reduced my intake of water. I could not sleep at night because of the turmoil in my mind.... Without saying anything to anyone, I set out toward the east... Then, heading in the direction of the holy place called Ghrishneshvara, near Ellora, I came upon the village of Nagad.... As I was looking around outside, my eye fell on a small *sādhanā* [ritual worship] hut. There had been a yogi doing sādhanā there before.... When I sat down inside the hut, my legs immediately folded into the lotus posture, and I started meditating. My beloved red aura came and stood before me, and then I heard a voice from within me, "Open that cupboard and read the book you find there"... I took it out and opened it. It opened at a page describing the very *kriyās* that had been happening to me. When I read it, I was supremely happy; in a moment, all my anguish, confusion and worry disappeared... I stayed in Nagad for some time, doing my sādhanā. Now I understood that the onset of sexual desire was connected with the process of becoming an *urdhvareta*, from which one gets the power to give Śaktipāt. When the Svādhisthāna chakra is pierced, sexual desire becomes very strong, but this happens so that the flow of sexual fluid may be turned upward and the sādhaka's lust destroyed forever.'[21]

In another recent autobiographical record, Gopi Krishna describes his experiences when Kuṇḍalinī was aroused spontaneously, without spiritual preparation or the guidance of a guru. Seated quietly in meditation one day he became aware of a strange and pleasing sensation below the base of the spine. The sensation came and went, until, with a 'roar like a waterfall', a stream of liquid light entered his brain through the spine and he became 'all consciousness' and 'immersed in a sea of light'. There followed restlessness and sufferings, however, and over the years Gopi Krishna continued to experience both visions of light and agonies of mind and body. He writes of one occasion that: 'The heat grew every moment, causing such unbearable pain that I writhed and twisted from side to side while streams of cold perspiration poured down my face and limbs. But still the heat increased and soon it seemed as if innumerable red-hot pins were coursing through my body, scorching and blistering the organs and tissues like flying sparks. Suffering the most excruciating torture, I clenched my hands and bit my lips to stop

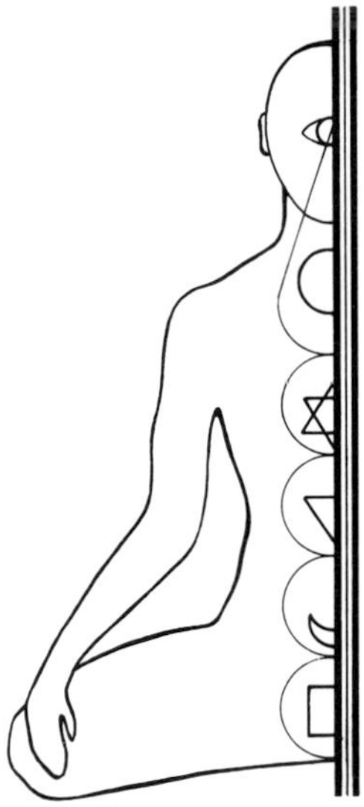

In the classical accounts, the physical symptoms of kuṇḍalinī-yoga begin at the base of the spine at the sacro-coccygeal plexus and involve the sacral plexus, the solar plexus, the cardiac plexus, the laryngeal plexus, the region of the pineal gland and the cerebral cortex

myself from leaping out of bed and crying at the top of my voice. The throbbing of my heart grew more and more terrific, acquiring such a spasmodic violence that I thought it must either stop beating or burst. Flesh and blood could not stand such strain, giving way any moment. It was easy to see that the body was valiantly trying to fight the virulent poison speeding across the nerves and pouring into the brain. But the fight was so unequal and the fury let loose in my system so lethal that there could not be the least doubt about the outcome. There was dreadful disturbance in all the organs, each so alarming and painful that I wonder how I managed to retain my self-possession under the onslaught. The whole delicate system was burning, withering away completely under the fiery blast racing through its interior.'

On a later occasion: 'There was no diminution in the vital radiation which, emanating from the seat of Kuṇḍalinī, sped across my nerves to every part of the body, filling my ears with strange sounds and my head with strange lights; but the current was now warm and pleasing instead of hot and burning, and it soothed and refreshed the tortured cells and tissues in a truly miraculous manner.... Whenever I turned my mental eye upon myself I invariably perceived a luminous glow within and outside my head in a state of constant vibration, as if a jet of an extremely subtle and brilliant substance rising through the spine spread itself out in the cranium, filling and surrounding it with an indescribable radiance. This shining halo never remained constant in dimension or in the intensity of its brightness. It waxed and waned, brightened and grew dim, or changed its colour from silver to gold and vice versa. When it increased in size or brilliance, the strange noise in my ears, now never absent, grew louder and more insistent, as if drawing my attention to something I could not understand. The halo was never stationary but in a state of perpetual motion, dancing and leaping, eddying and swirling, as if composed of innumerable, extremely subtle, brilliant particles of some immaterial substance, shooting up and down, this way and that, combining to present an appearance of a circling, shimmering pool of light.'[22]

Ramakrishna, who followed the disciplines of kuṇḍalinī-yoga under the guidance of a female guru, Brāhmaṇī, achieved in three days the result promised by each of the rituals. He described his experience as a hopping, pushing up, moving zig-zag. He directly perceived the ascent of the Kuṇḍalinī, and later described to his disciples its various movements as fishlike, birdlike, monkeylike, and so on. He spoke of the centres of energy from his own experience in this way: 'In the Scriptures mention is made of the seven centres of consciousness. When the mind is attached to worldliness, con-

Opposite: the ascending planes from the unconscious to relative consciousness to Cosmic Consciousness

sciousness dwells in the three lower centres, the plexus, sacro-coccygeal, sacral, and solar. Then there are in it no high ideals or pure thoughts. It remains immersed in lust and greed. The fourth centre of consciousness is the region of the heart. Spiritual awakening comes when the mind rises to this centre. At this stage man has a spiritual vision of the Divine Light and is struck with wonder at its beauty and glory. His mind then no longer runs after worldly pleasures. The region of the throat is the fifth centre of consciousness. When mind rises to this centre, man becomes free from nescience and ignorance. He then talks only on subjects relating to God and grows impatient if any worldly topic is discussed. He avoids hearing about worldly subjects. When mind rises to the sixth centre between the eyebrows, man becomes merged in divine consciousness. There is still left in him, however, the consciousness of a separate ego. Seeing the beatific vision of God he becomes mad with joy and longs to come closer to him and be united with him. But he cannot, for there is still the ego which stands between them. One may compare God to the light in a lantern. You seem to feel its warmth, yet though you wish to do so, you cannot touch it, on account of the glass intervening. The centre in the brain is the seventh centre. When one rises to this plane, there is *samādhi.* That is the transcendental consciousness, in which one realizes his oneness with God.'[23]

Ramakrishna tried to describe the details of his Kuṇḍalinī experience to his close disciples: 'I'll tell you everything today and will not keep anything secret.' Pointing to the spot between the eyebrows he said: 'The Supreme Self is directly known and the individual experiences samādhi when the mind comes here. There remains then but a thin transparent screen separating the Supreme Self and the individual self. The sādhaka then experiences...'. Saying this, at the moment he started to describe in detail the realization of the Supreme Self, he was plunged in samādhi. When the samādhi came to an end, he tried again to describe the realization of the Supreme Self and was again in samādhi.

After several fruitless attempts, he broke down in tears. 'Well, I sincerely wish to tell you everything... without concealing anything whatsoever,' but he was unable to speak. 'Who should speak? The very distinction between 'I' and 'thou' vanishes: Whenever I try to describe what kinds of visions I experience when it goes beyond this place [showing the throat] and think what kinds of visions I am witnessing, the mind rushes immediately up, and speaking becomes impossible.' In the final centre, 'the distinction between the subject of consciousness and the object of consciousness is destroyed. It is a state wherein self-identity and the field of consciousness are blended in one indissoluble whole.[24]

The whole world was revealed to Ramakrishna as the play of Śiva-Śakti. The barrier between the matter and energy broke down for him, and he saw even a grain of sand and a blade of grass as vibrating with energy. The universe appeared to him as a lake of mercury or of silver, and he had a vision of the ultimate cause of the universe as a huge luminous triangle giving birth every moment to an infinite number of universes.

Dhyanyogi observes that: 'We do not all have identical experiences in meditation. In our path of meditation, one should not aim at such uniformity. Everyone's experiences are conditioned by his previous impressions or saṃskāras. It sometimes happens in the knowledge of the sādhaka that, after Śaktipāt [energy-moving], all the six chakras or lotuses are pierced by the uprising Kuṇḍalinī and he goes into samādhi. Sometimes he remains unaware of the piercing of the six chakras, possibly because the kriyās [involuntary movements occasioned in the human body under the effect of yoga] caused by it are perfunctory and minimal.'[25]

During non-meditative Kuṇḍalinī arousal, all the chakras may be experienced simultaneously, since the highest state embraces all former experience. Ramakrishna relates how: 'One day in June or July, when I was six or seven years old, I was walking along a narrow path separating the paddy fields, eating some of the puffed rice which I was carrying in a basket, and looking up at the sky I saw a beautiful, sombre thunder-cloud. As it spread, rapidly enveloping the whole sky, a flight of snow-white cranes flew overhead in front of it. It presented such a beautiful contrast that my mind wandered to far off regions. Lost to outward sense, I fell down, and the rice was scattered in all directions. Some people found me in that plight and carried me home in their arms. That was the first time I completely lost consciousness in ecstasy.' Throughout his life 'God-consciousness' was easily awakened in him, and plunged him into samādhi. Later in his life, a glimpse of an English boy leaning against a tree with his body bent in three places like the traditional pictures of Krishna, sent him into 'communion with God'.

On another occasion his mystical vision arose from despair. Ramakrishna became the priest of the Kālī Temple, north of Calcutta, and when one day, after going through meditational spiritual practices, he could not achieve the desired goal, he prayed to the Divine Mother Kālī: 'Are you real or are you a delusion? Am I making a fool of myself imagining that I can ever know you?' He began to suffer excruciating physical pain and great restlessness. 'I could not bear the separation any longer; life did not seem worth living. Suddenly my eyes fell on the sword that was kept in the Mother's temple. Determined to put an end to my life, I jumped up

like a madman and seized it, when suddenly the blessed Mother revealed herself to me and I fell unconscious on the floor. The buildings with their different parts, the temple, and everything else vanished from my sight, leaving no trace whatsoever. Instead I saw a limitless, infinite, effulgent Ocean of Bliss. As far as the eye could see, the shining billows were madly rushing towards me on all sides with a terrific noise to swallow me up. I was panting for breath. I was caught in the rush and collapsed, unconscious. What was happening in the outside world I did not know; but within me there was a steady flow of undiluted bliss, altogether new, and I felt the presence of the Divine Mother.' Colin Wilson comments that 'Long meditation had tired him until he had lost sight of his aim. The decision to kill himself was a sudden danger to his vital power that aroused all his sleeping life-energies.'[26]

Devī as an enchantress of the universe – Mahāmāyā – the enchantment of illusory 'reality' that must be cast off in meditative practice. Pahari School, c. 18th century, gouache on paper

Supernatural powers are one of the manifestations associated with the practice of kuṇḍalinī-yoga, and they may also appear following spontaneous arousal of the Kuṇḍalinī energy. Self-actualization may be manifested in such special attainments (siddhis) as living without food, duplicating one's body, rising from the dead, gaining knowledge of the 'heavenly worlds, of the planets, stars, universes and the whole cosmos', weightlessness, levitation and travel through space. The accounts of the lives of the famous tantric Nātha yogis contain numerous descriptions of such accomplishments. Popular tradition holds that the saints of the Nātha cult are still living in their subtle, supra-material bodies in the remote Himalayas or forests. In recent years a well-known tantric scholar, Dr Gopinath Kaviraj, came across some of these yogis and recorded his personal experiences with them.[27] Jyotiji is a yogi who frequently travels in space after leaving his material body. Kedarnath is a young boy who is similarly gifted with the power of leaving behind his earthly body and travelling to remote regions. After his return, he is able to describe his experiences. At first his parents and his friends believed that he was mentally ill and tried various treatments. But the boy insisted that he left his body in full consciousness, and that his memory was intact after his return from his space-odyssey.

The onset of his strange experience was recorded by Dr Kaviraj. One day, near Daśāsvamedha Ghāt market in Banaras, Kedar noticed a curious figure with a red body, staring at him. Suddenly the man touched him and then disappeared. Kedar returned home with a high fever. In his febrile state he saw his father and his father's guru, both of whom were dead. They asked him to leave his body and come out, and, by means of some inexplicable energy he was able to do so.

With meditative practice, Kedar could see a radiance of light all around. Highly subtle movement of the body-energy became possible. He attained all the different stages, and could travel through celestial spheres by applying the unusual forces he possessed.

There is abundant evidence that their yogic powers enabled the siddhāi-yogis to defy gravity. Though not transformed into incorporeal beings, they attained a buoyancy which reduced their body weight and allowed them to lift themselves in space as they pleased. Mental concentration on cosmic energy reaches a stage when the yogi feels so light that he can travel 'resting his etheric body even on sunbeams'. Although they may arise in the course of kuṇḍalinī-yoga, these supernatural powers are seen by tantrikas as impediments to the attainment of the higher consciousness and liberation.

To the present there has been little systematic clinical study or scientific investigation of the Kuṇḍalinī phenomena, although certain discrepancies between the classical descriptions of Kuṇḍalinī experience and modern clinical findings have led Western researchers to propose a 'physio-kundalini' model to account for their observations. This concept has been derived from a model proposed by Itzhak Bentov, an American researcher who approached the problem of altered states of consciousness through studies of the effects of vibration-frequencies on human physiology.

That a sequence of unusually strong physiological reactions accompanies the rise of Kuṇḍalinī we already know from Tantric texts, from which we also learn to expect a series of unusual psychological changes. Most meditators understand these to be the effect of the meditation process and so are not unduly alarmed. However, among non-meditators or among socio-cultural groups who do not have access to information about Kuṇḍalinī energy, similar reactions may be triggered off by environmental stimuli. The experiments of Bentov[28] show that exposure to certain mechanical vibration, electromagnetic waves or sonic vibration can be responsible. The resultant symptoms, presented for medical attention, have not till recently been fully recognized or understood for what they are. It is Itzhak Bentov who in his various experiments indicates that far from being a neurotic aberration, these 'kundalini' states indicate an alteration in consciousness linked to alterations in bodily rhythm and bio-magnetic field.

Bentov's observations (using a ballistocardiogram) of the seated subject engaged in deep meditation reveal a rhythmic sine wave pattern. He attributes this to the development during the course of meditation of a 'standing wave' in the aorta, the main artery from the heart, that is reflected in rhythmic motion of the body. This resonating oscillator – the heart-aorta system – in turn 'entrains' further bio-oscillators – the brain, the cerebral ventricles and the sensory cortex of the brain – which together effect a modification of the cerebral magnetic field.

This co-ordinated system activates a travelling stimulus, an oscillating 'current', in the sensory cortex tissue, which is finally polarized to a point where each hemisphere of the brain produces a pulsating magnetic field. Bentov writes: 'This magnetic field – radiated by the head acting as an antenna – interacts with the electric and magnetic fields already in the environment. We may consider the head as simultaneously a transmitting and receiving antenna, tuned to a particular one of the several resonant frequencies of the brain.'

Bentov suggests that the 'kundalini' effect may be regarded as part of a development of the nervous system: 'We can postulate that our magnetic 'antennae' will bring in information about our extended system – the planet and the sun – and will allow us to interpret geophysical phenomena and signals to better advantage.'

Describing the sequence of bodily sensations experienced by his subjects in association with the 'sensory motor cortex syndrome' or 'kundalini process', Bentov writes of 'a transient paresthesia of the toes or ankle with numbness and tingling. Occasionally, there is diminished sensitivity to touch or pain, or even partial paralysis

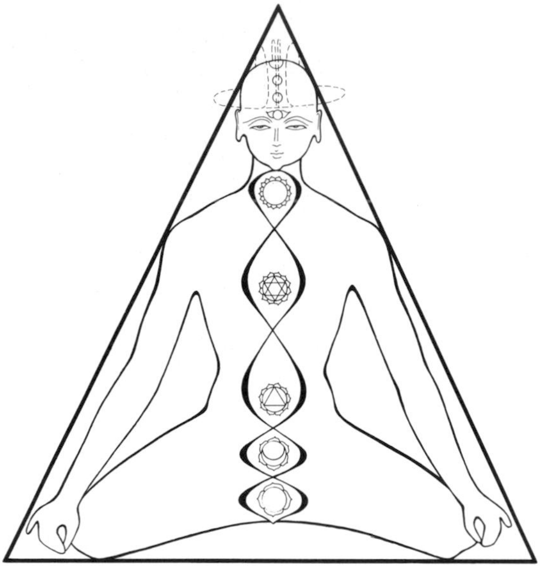

Pulsating magnetic fields developing around the hemispheres of the brain during deep meditation

of the foot or leg. The process most frequently begins on the left side and ascends in a sequential manner from foot, leg, hip, to involve completely the left side of the body, including the face. Once the hip is involved, it is not uncommon to experience an intermittent throbbing or rhythmic rumbling-like sensation in the lower lumbar and sacral spine. This is followed by an ascending sensation which rises along the spine to the cervical and occipital regions of the head.'

The building up of pressure at head and neck may signal itself in an aching sensation, usually transient, sometimes persistent. Similar pressure may be felt along the spine, the thorax and up to the head and eyes. Tingling may then descend from the face to the throat, while there is a sense of air-pressure rushing to and fro between thoractic cavity and throat. Breathing becomes spasmodic, with emphatic expiration. A high-pitched hum or ringing in the ears may be experienced, together with visual disturbance, or a decrease or temporary loss of vision. The sense of internal change eventually recedes to the abdomen.

Bentov points to the stimulation of the sensory cortex by the circulating 'current' as offering a possible physiological explanation for the sequence of symptoms of the 'awakened Kuṇḍalinī'. Further: 'As the stimulus travels through, it crosses an area which contains a pleasure centre. When the pleasure centre is thus stimulated, the meditator experiences a state of ecstasy. To reach that 'state' it may take years of systematic meditation, or again, in certain people, it may happen spontaneously.'

All the characteristic elements of the Kuṇḍalinī experience are included in the classical descriptions, yet these descriptions differ

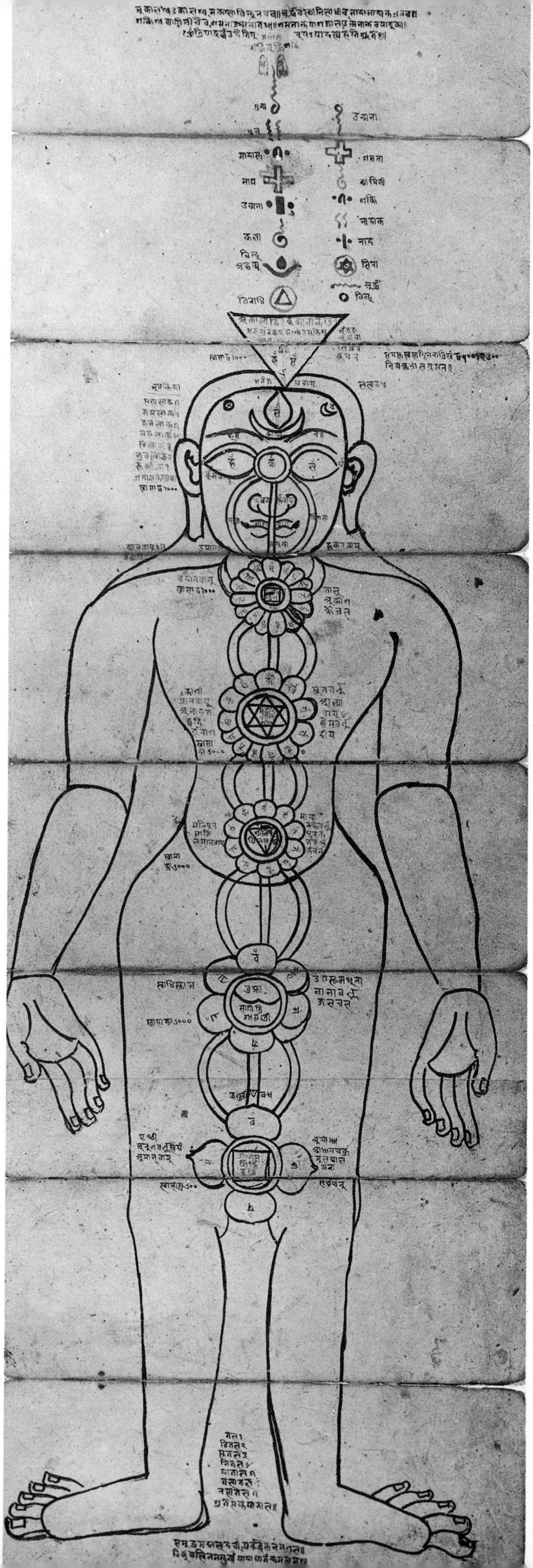

The levels extending beyond Sahasrāra chakra. Nepal, c. 19th century, ink on paper

in some respects from modern clinical observations. It has been found by researchers that the 'energy sensation' travels up the legs to the spine to the top of the head, then down the face, through the throat, to a terminal point in the abdomen, whereas in the classic descriptions the energy awakens at the base of the spine, travels up the spinal canal, and has completed its journey when it reaches the top of the head.

The classical description of Kuṇḍalinī awakening at the base of the spine is similarly at variance with the experience described by Ramakrishna, that 'something rises with a tingling sensation from the feet to the head'. This disparity may be resolved by the traditional representations of kuṇḍalinī-yoga, particularly in old scroll-paintings. The depths of the unconscious are generally depicted as the gigantic serpent Śesha, meaning 'residue', so named because it was born from what remained after the creation of the Three Worlds. Śesha's thousand heads are expanded into a mighty hood, and it forms the couch of Vishṇu as Nārāyaṇa who reclines on its coils in trance-sleep. Scroll paintings illustrating kuṇḍalinī-yoga depict only the Śesha, which is also identified with Ananta, 'endless'. An archetype of the unconscious, it rises from the depth of the primeval waters and, passing through Vishṇu's early manifestations or 'descents', as Matsya or fish, Kūrma or tortoise, Varāha or boar, touches human beings and only then comes to the Mūlādhāra or base chakra, the controlling centre which cannot be by-passed, where it lies in the dormant state until its unfolding.

These paintings also illustrate the concept that when Kuṇḍalinī reaches the highest chakra, Sahasrāra, the process does not stop: it becomes supra-mental as one enters the seven higher stages of consciousness, participating in the greatest cosmic adventure – an experiential journey of the expansion of human consciousness. 'Beginning with the sixth chakra, the Ājñā chakra, consciousness *starts* to go trans-personal. Consciousness is now going trans-verbal *and* trans-personal....This is total and utter transcendence and release into Formless Consciousness, Boundless Radiance. There is here no self, no God, no final-God, no subjects, and no thingness, apart from other than Consciousness as Such....Each step is an increase in consciousness and an identification of Awareness until all forms return to perfect and radical release in Formlessness.'[29]

According to Kashmir Śaivism, the highest Reality, which is nothing but *chaitanya* (Pure Consciousness), is Paramaśiva. The illustrations depict these various planes in ascending order: Bindu, Ardhacandra, Rodhinī, Nāda, Nādānta, Śakti, Vyāpikā, Nirvāṇa, Unmanī and finally the ultimate state of Mahābindu (the supra-cosmic and metacosmic Void), 'a void containing everything' in

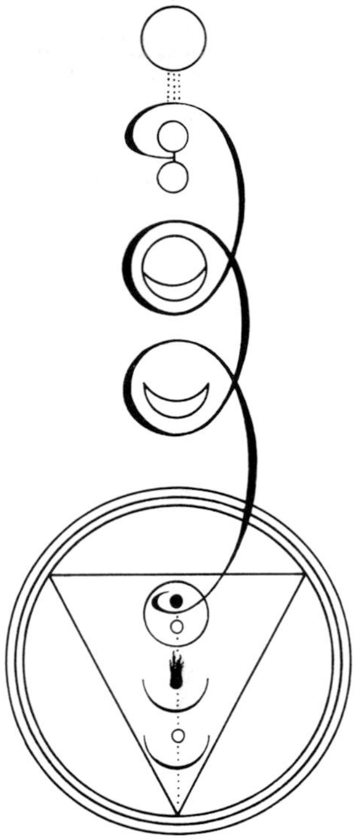

Opposite: diagram of the chakras and their presiding deities and śaktis, and the energy channels of the feet and legs. Nepal, contemporary, gouache on paper

Above: stages of energy transformation, through 'trans-verbal' and 'trans-personal' levels to release into the Void

Lao-Tzu's phrase, An aspirant of kuṇḍalinī-yoga must penetrate these stages of consciousness to reach the supraconscious level. The realization of Mahābindu or Parābindu (the transcendental Void) is possible only after the awakening of Kuṇḍalinī.

Commenting on the system of chakras according to the famous Nāthayogi Goraknātha (*c.* AD 1120), Dr Kaviraj writes that beyond this is a series of twenty voids. 'The ms. [*Devatā Acintyanātha and the Śakti Avyaktā*] observes that the final liberation takes place in the great void (paramaśunya-sthāna) above twenty-one brahmāṇḍas. Transcending the great void the Yogin becomes eternally free from 'coming and going', i.e. the wheel of birth and death.'[30]

One should not, however, understand from the above statements that the different stages or parts of the Kuṇḍalinī process take place, as it were, externally: they are intimately connected with the broader system, and the progression is within the whole, i.e., within Sahasrāra.

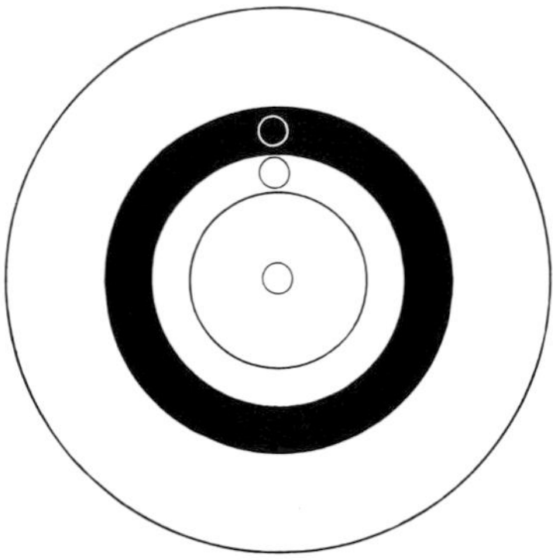

All levels are contained within the Sahasrāra: from the centre, the Mahābindu within the Sahasrāra maṇḍala, the sphere of the superconscious (Cit); next, Rajabindu within the Tatastha maṇḍala, symbolizing the empirical mind in the higher consciousness (Chitta-ākāsa) containing billions of galaxies; next, Tamabindu (tama = black) within the Māyā maṇḍala, symbolizing the phenomenal worlds (Bhūta-ākāsa) encircled within the Whole

XIII *Vishṇu reclining on the primordial serpent-power, Śesha or Ananta, symbolizing the Supreme Being in a state of cosmic slumber, the unconscious or the underworld. From the navel of Vishṇu emerges Brahmā the creator, encountering the negative forces in the chaotic waters of the dissolved cosmos. Kangra School, c. 18th century, gouache on paper*

XIV *Within the folds of Devī, the Cosmic Energy, rests Śiva, the foundational Consciousness. Devī (or Kuṇḍalinī) is the primordial power active in the great drama of the awakening of the unmanifested Siva. Pahari School, c. 18th century, gouache on paper*

The *Yoga Upanishad* explains the organization of the chakras as embracing the whole body starting with the feet: from the feet to the knees is the region of earth element; from the knees to the anus, the water element; from the anus to the heart, the fire element; from heart to the middle of the eyebrows, the air element; from the centre of the eyebrows to the top of the head, the ether element where it is circular in shape, smoky-white in colour, and vibrating with the letter Ha (= Śakti).

The symptoms of the Kuṇḍalinī phenomena are of variable duration. With some individuals a specific symptom may linger for months or even years. The full symptomatic sequence may not appear immediately obvious, or may not seem to follow connectedly. As a result, the whole process has frequently been dismissed as a psychosomatic or neurotic disturbance, and, owing to the general lack of understanding of its nature, drastic and unnecessary treatment, as for schizophrenia or other mental illness, has been resorted to.

XIII

XIV

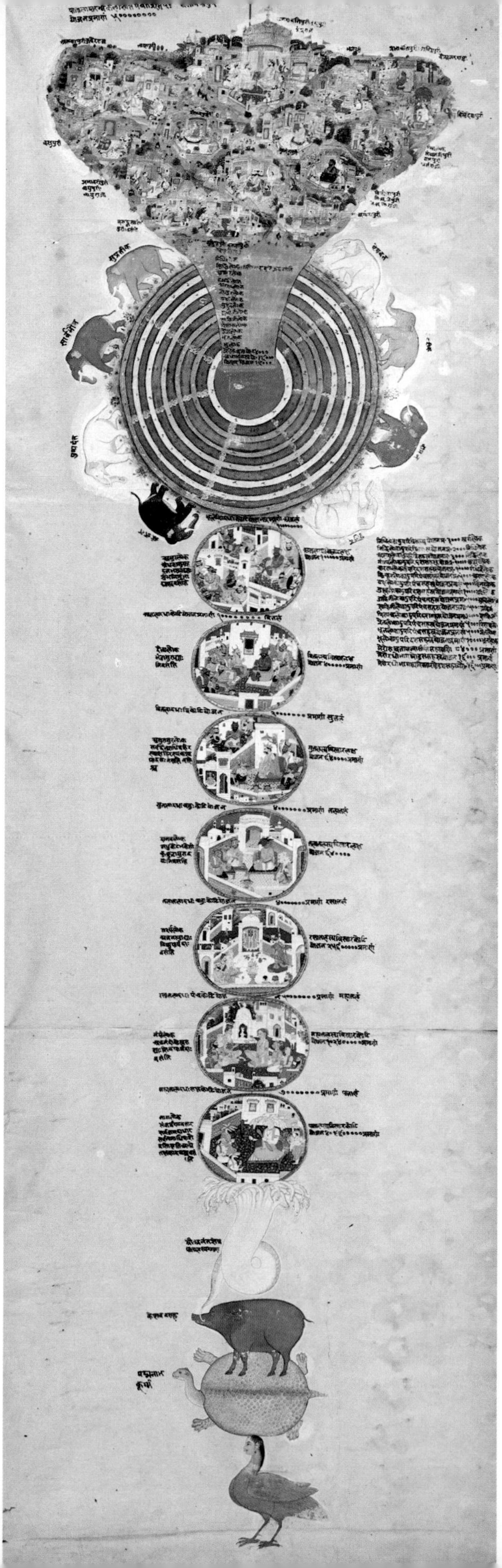

XV

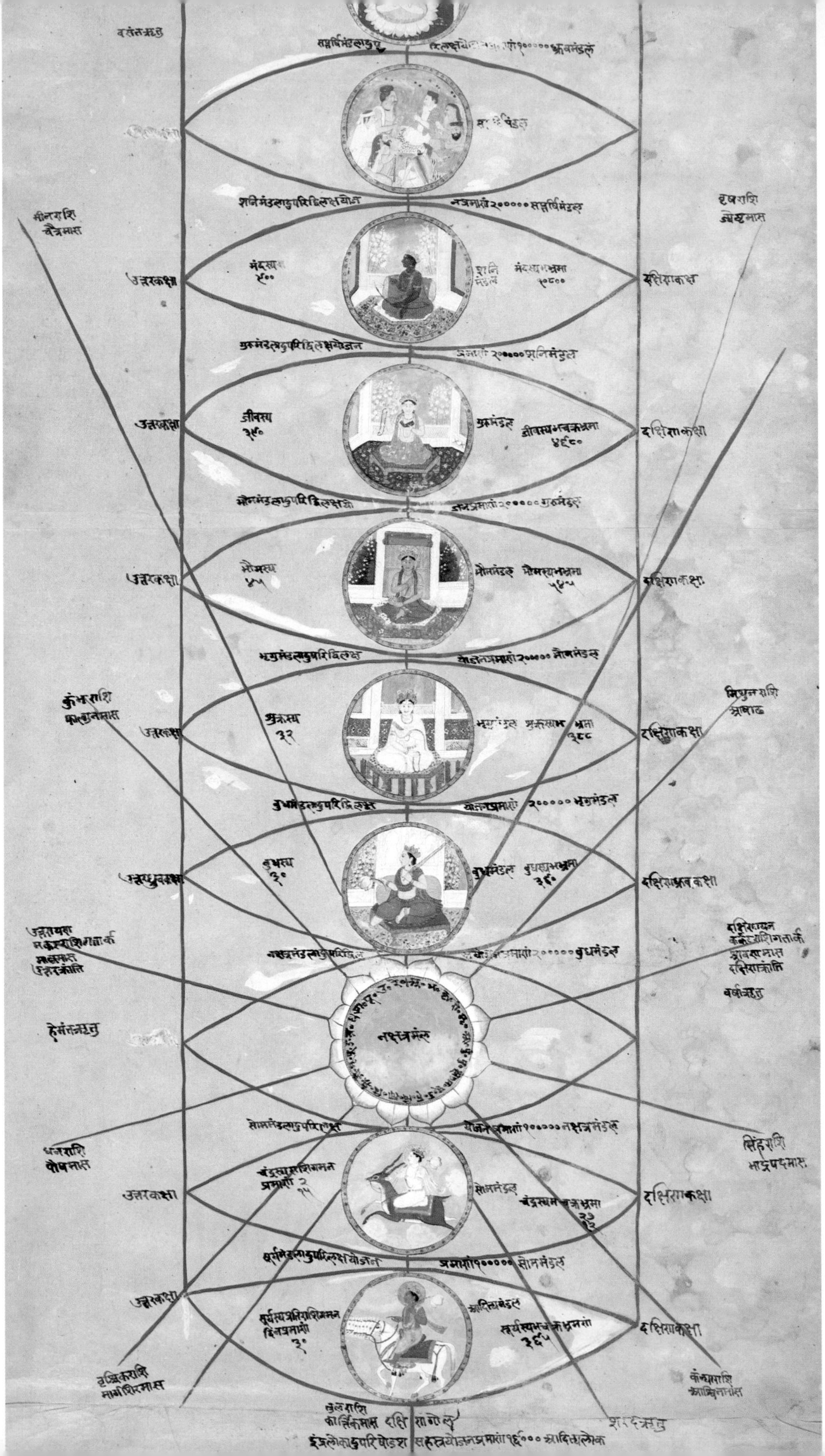

XVI

0 ● Mahābindu (the Absolute Void)

9 Unmanī (superconsciousness - beyond mind) Śiva-tattva

8 Nirvāṇa (Samanā) ⎫
                 ⎬ Śakti-tattva
7 Vyāpikā (Vyāpinī) ⎭

6 Kalā (Śakti) ⎫

5 Nādānta ⎬ Creative pulsation of sound and light

4 Nāda ⎭

3 ▽ Rodhinī (Nirodhikā) Subtle energy of sound

2 Ardhacandra (Ardhendu) The half-moon light/subtle energy

1 Bindu (point) Compact mass of energy projecting itself/the
                        two poles: zero and infinity

↑
Higher Levels of Consciousness

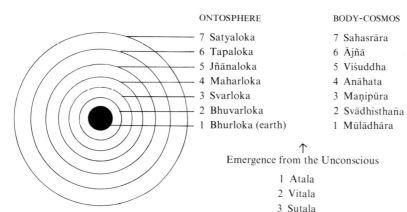

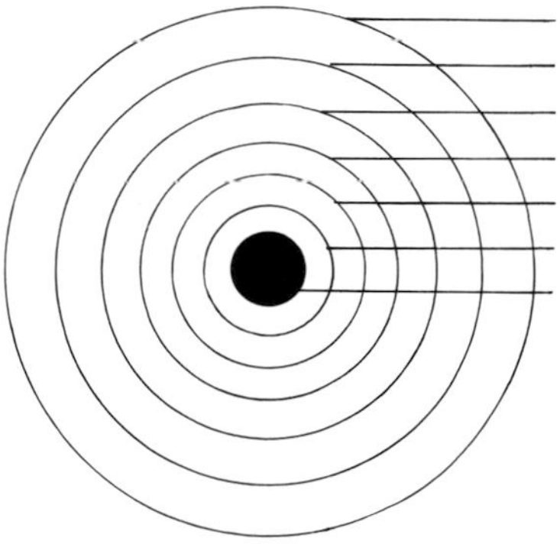

ONTOSPHERE	BODY-COSMOS
7 Satyaloka	7 Sahasrāra
6 Tapaloka	6 Ājñā
5 Jñānaloka	5 Viśuddha
4 Maharloka	4 Anāhata
3 Svarloka	3 Maṇipūra
2 Bhuvarloka	2 Svādhisthaṇa
1 Bhurloka (earth)	1 Mūlādhāra

↑
Emergence from the Unconscious

1 Atala
2 Vitala
3 Sutala
4 Talātala
5 Mahātala
6 Rasātala
7 Pātāla

*From below: the seven talas,
subterranean regions of the unconscious,
from which the Serpent-Power emerges
and ascends through the relative worlds,
beginning with Bhurloka (earth).
According to Kashmir Śaivism, the
cosmos reverts through higher levels of
consciousness to the AbsoluteVoid, which
is the ultimate unified field, the
Mahābindu (Śiva-Śakti), the very source
and essence of all life*

*XV The evolution of the
universe from the lowest gross
matter to the earth-sphere.
Kangra School, c. 18th century
gouache on paper*

*XVI Above the underworld
and the earth-sphere, the
cosmic energy passes through
the planetary and astrological
chakras, towards the realm of
Pure Experience, the chakras
of union and bliss. Kangra
School, c. 18th century, gouache
on paper*

Writing of the variations in Kuṇḍalinī experience, another American researcher, Lee Sannella, has observed that, 'if we accept the view that they are the results of the balancing action of Kundalini as it removes blocks throughout the system, then individual differences in symptom-patterns mean that separate areas are blocked. This may be due to differences in genetic make-up and past history of the persons. Also, these processes may last from a few months to several years. Such differences in time-span may be caused by variation in the intensity of meditation and in the total amount of balancing needed.... This arrest of the physio-kundalini cycle may occur in those who become fascinated with some particular psychic ability. Such an exclusive focus may intercept the progression at that particular stage. Further variation occurs over a period of time; the signs and symptoms are not present continuously but come on at intervals, most often in meditation, during quiet time or in sleep.'[31]

Dr Sannella further observes that: 'We find quite 'ordinary' people who complete the physio-kundalini cycle in a matter of months, whereas yogic scriptures assign a minimum of three years for the culmination of full kundalini awakening in the case of the most advanced initiates.' Here again, as we have seen, there can be no hard and fast rules. Ramakrishna achieved realization within three days from initiation, and there are plenty of similar cases. Probably, as Dr Sannella proposes: 'Kundalini plays a much larger part in daily life than most of us have hitherto supposed; there is a far lower and gentler manifestation of it which is already awake within us all, which is not only innocuous but beneficent, which is doing its appointed work day and night while we are entirely unconscious of its presence and activity.'[32] He also suggests that the 'physio-kundalini' mechanism may be a separate entity, which can be activated as a part of a full Kuṇḍalinī awakening.

A representative account of an experience of Kuṇḍalinī taking place over a long period of time was given to the author by a young American woman writer. According to her, 'it was in an all-involving attempt to understand the various experiences and symptoms which had been dominating my life that I came upon ancient and modern descriptions of the Kundalini awakening and realized that they explained what had been happening to me. I understand now, in retrospect, that I first felt the energies when I was entering puberty. The process was not too demanding until the birth of my first child. I had been practising Hatha Yoga intensively and previous to the delivery had been unknowingly training daily with childbirth preparation methods that were very close to the yogic pranayama exercises. During the labor and delivery, tremendous energy was released and there were powerful visions of light. The reaction of those around me was to stop it with tranquilizers as quickly as possible. Several years later, after semi-successfully suppressing it, I met Swami Muktananda; it was at a time that I neither knew or cared about spiritual teachers and yet the experience around him was so compelling that I knew I had to pursue it. It was then that the Kundalini process became a daily, encompassing phenomenon in my life, no longer to be denied. It was accelerated by a serious automobile accident in which there was a powerful experience of dying and moving beyond death into a timeless sense of unity and peace.

'For the past five years, I have been aware of the Kundalini energy daily and it has taken many forms, some of them expansive and elevating, many of them disturbing and difficult. I feel that the tremendous force of the Kundalini Shakti has been cascading through my entire physical, emotional, spiritual system, detecting and breaking up knots of stored experience or emotion; as the contents of these blocked areas (sequences from childhood, from birth, from transpersonal realms) come into consciousness, there are powerful visual experiences, emotional releases, severe physical symptoms, and existential insights. Much of the physical activity has occurred on the left side of the body; there was cramping in the legs, rushing energy from the base of the spine up the back, often jamming in the neck and shoulder area. Once those symptoms were cleared, the focus was around the eyes, producing oppressive headaches, inability to read, and occasional blindness. Often there

A Western representation of Kuṇḍalinī experience. Contemporary, gouache on paper

was a feeling of activity in the sinuses and constriction in the throat. For many months, the energy concentrated on the area of the abdomen and the ovaries, creating a great deal of physical pain and nausea.

'The progression of the Kundalini has been almost linear (from the legs, up the back, to the top of the neck, over the top of the head into the eyes, to the throat and into the stomach and female organ); as the energy finally clears an area, the symptoms disappear and do not return. At times, I can feel a specific chakra being activated, and at others, especially when the energies are particularly powerful, it feels as though the whole chakra system is being worked on. There have often been violent tremors, automatic movements and breathing, and searing heat throughout my system. I have felt extremely sensitive and receptive, sometimes taking on the symptoms or energies of those around me or experiencing accurate psychic impressions. There have been recurring visions of serpents, beautiful ecstatic states of intense light, and a sense of rich, healing energy travelling along thousands of tiny channels throughout my system.

'By trial and error I have learned the circumstances under which the Kundalini activity will sometimes be accelerated. For many months, the practice of any meditative techniques, Hatha yoga, or fasting produced uncomfortable and chaotic states. A vibratory field, such as that of a large city or a moving jet airplane, has guaranteed increased activity, as has contact with an advanced spiritual teacher. Sometimes, there is a build-up of what feels to be a karmic pattern, involving amazing synchronistic events and a resolution which is accompanied by explosive energy release. But most of the time, the Kundalini seems to establish its own pace at will, without my control or consent. There has not been a day in the past years that I have not been aware of it, although some periods are more intense than others.'

A case history is used by Dr Sannella to illustrate what he and his co-researchers believe to be the most typical pattern of 'physio-kundalini'. He records that a forty-eight-year-old woman artist 'started transcendental meditation, and after about five years began to experience occasional tingling in her arms and heat in her hands. She did not sleep for days, with energy surging through her whole body, and had several dreams of having her consciousness separated from her body. A continuous loud sound had appeared inside her head. Soon there were cramps in her big toes, followed by vibratory feelings in her legs. Overnight, her big toe nails darkened, as if hit by a hammer, and eventually partially separated from the flesh. The tissues in her legs felt torn through by vibratory sensations.

The vibrations spread to her lower back and swept over her body from lower back up to her head, forming a sensation of a band around the head, just above the eyebrows. Then her head started to move spontaneously. Later her body moved sinuously and her tongue pressed to the roof of her mouth. Then she sensed a strong sound of 'om' there. The tinglings spread back of her neck and head, over the head to her forehead and face. Both nostrils were stimulated, causing a feeling of elongation of the nose. The tinglings then spread down her face. At times her eyes seemed to move separately, and the pupils felt like holes that bored into her head and met in the center. Then she felt a tremendous head pressure and a brilliant light, followed by bliss and laughter. The tinglings spread further down to her upper lip, chin, and mouth. About this time there were dreams of heavenly music. Then the sensations went to her throat, chest and abdomen, and eventually she felt as if there was a closing of the circuit in the shape of an egg; up through the spine, down through the front of the body. As it developed, the circuit activated particular chakras on its way; starting in the lower abdomen, then the navel, the solar plexus, the heart, then the head centers. The last to be activated was the throat. After that there was a continuous feeling of energy pouring into the body through the navel area. This feeling stopped after the circuit was completed. The whole experience had strong sexual overtones. The greater part of this activity occurred over several months. In the last two years there has been only occasional activity, mostly during meditation, or when she is relaxed in bed.

'During the experience there was spontaneous yogic breathing (faint and controlled). Eventually there developed head pressures, which centered around the back of the head, the top and the forehead. These pressures would become especially severe during reading, resulting in discomfort around the eyes and a pulsing sensation at the top of the head.

'The loud sound inside the head eventually disappeared. Throughout the experience she understood that she was undergoing the rising of kundalini, because she had read about it before. Therefore, she felt relaxed about it and just allowed things to happen. However, she became emotionally perturbed, and had difficulty in integrating these experiences with her daily activities.

'Since the inflow of energy prevented normal sleep for months and continued during the day as well, work became inefficient, and she felt as if she was completely detached and was witnessing her own activities. Eventually, she brought the situation under control. The general effect was a greater emotional stability and elimination of tension, along with a greatly enhanced intuitive insight.'

Dr Sannella writes of the benefits for his patients of the physio-kundalini process that: 'Each one of our own cases is now successful on his or her own terms. They all report that they handle stress more easily, and are more fulfilled than ever before in relationships with others.... But in the initial stages, the stress of the experience itself, coupled with a negative attitude from oneself or others, may be overwhelming and cause severe imbalance....'

'Symptoms, when caused by this process, will disappear spontaneously in time. Because it is essentially a purificatory or balancing process, and each person has only a finite amount of impurities of the sort removed by kundalini, the process is self-limiting. Disturbances seen are therefore not pathological, but rather therapeutic, constituting a removal of potentially pathological elements. The kundalini force arises spontaneously from deep within the mind, and is apparently self-directing. Tension and imbalance thus result, not from the process itself, but from conscious or subconscious interference with it. Helping the person to understand and accept what is happening to him or to her may be the best that we can do.

'Usually the process, left to itself, will find its own natural pace and balance. But if it has already become too rapid and violent, our experience suggests it may be advisable to take steps such as heavier diet, suspension of meditations, and vigorous physical activity, to moderate its course.

'The people in whom the physio-kundalini process is most easily activated, and in whom it is most likely to be violent and disturbing, are those with especially sensitive nervous systems – the natural psychics. Many of our cases had some psychic experience prior to their awakening. Natural psychics often find the physio-kundalini experience so intense that they will not engage in the regular classical meditation methods that usually further the kundalini process; instead, they either refrain from meditation or adopt some mild form of their own devising. But much of their anxiety may be due to misunderstanding and ignorance of the physio-kundalini process. Rather than increasing their fear, we should be giving them the knowledge and confidence to allow the process to progress at the maximum comfortable, natural rate.'[33]

David Tansley recently reported on 'radionic' methods of diagnosis primarily concerned with the utilization of subtle force fields and energies in the human organism. 'Chakras', he writes, 'can be damaged by traumatic accidents, and especially by sudden, dramatic, emotional shocks. Nagging fears or anxiety can, through constant wearing activity, disturb the functional balance. Chakras are frequently found to be blocked, either at the point where energy enters, or at the point where it exits to flow into the etheric body.

If a blockage occurs at the entrance, the energy flowing in is frequently driven back to its point of origin on the astral or mental planes. This brings about psychological problems and endocrine disfunction. If the blockage is at the exit, the energy builds up until enough pressure enables it to burst through to stimulate the appropriate endocrine gland. This causes erratic endocrine function with attendant physical and psychological problems.'[34]

The development of 'radionic' therapeutic measures was started in 1933, and carried on by the late George de la Warr and his wife at their laboratories at Oxford, from 1945. David Tansley in 1972 related radionics to the chakras. He points out that 'these chakras are of vital importance to the practitioner, because they are the focal points which receive energies for the purpose of vitalizing the physical body.... These centres are in the nature of distributing agencies, providing dynamic force and qualitative energy to the man. They produce definite effects upon his outward physical appearance, and through their continuous activity his character tendencies emerge.'[35]

Through radionic exposure, it has been found that all objects, whether animate or inanimate, emanate energy. A Radionics 'Mark III Centre' instrument has been evolved by David Tansley in order to treat directly the chakras of the etheric anatomy. 'Over the years radionics has developed a catalogue of the specific vibrationary frequencies (or 'rates'), expressed in numbers, not only of the essential aetheric 'radio stations' in the body – the chakras – but also of the specific diseases which we allow to enter our systems. ... In this respect the radionics box can be seen as a twentieth-century mediumistic device, an electronic 'crystal ball' through which man's intuitive, as well as rational, faculties are given equal rein. Radionics is thus a further point of fusion between the spheres of science and occultism, through whose narrow connecting point can be seen the developing terrain of interior knowledge.'[36]

If the 'impurities' or 'imbalances' or 'blockages' have any objective reality, it should be possible to demonstrate them, Dr Sannella suggests, with physiological and psychological tests, and to correlate their removal with specific signs and symptoms observed clinically. 'We did an interesting experiment – using H. Motoyama's electric field sensor, or "chakra measuring device". When the subject sat quietly in this machine, we could observe the usual EEG waveform. After a few minutes of deep meditation, probably at the point where he feels he has transcended, there suddenly appeared a diminution of these signals, and a corresponding increase in amplitude in a higher frequency band, one which our experimenters had not been equiped to detect. To our surprise, this new waveform

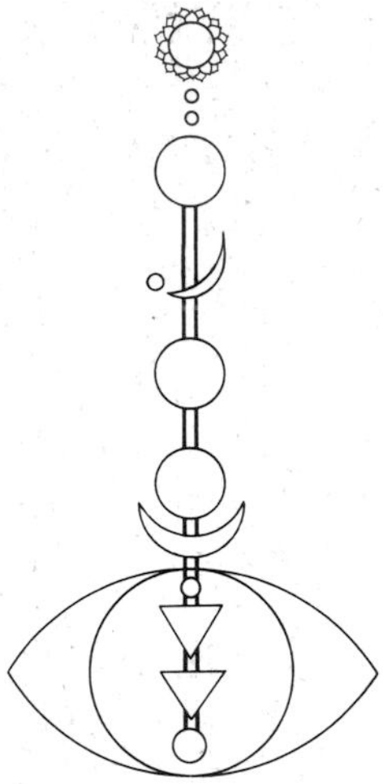

From Ājñā, each step (ten in Kashmir Śaivism) is an increase in consciousness and an identification, until all forms return to the great Void of Sahasrāra (see p. 89)

The explosion of psychic energy in the subtle body of a yogi after he has surmounted the levels of existence. South India, c. 1900, gouache on paper

was in the frequency range of 350 to 500 Hz, much higher than the 0-to-50 Hz frequency range of a normal EEG waveform. These higher frequency EEG signals could be an easily measured physiological indicator of certain meditative states and out-of-the-body experiences, or bilocation of consciousness. If so, a subject full of mystery and fascination for centuries now becomes a new frontier for researchers.'[37]

Here, however, research is still in its infancy.

There are, however, two important facts to keep in mind while research and investigation continues. One is that panic is only experienced by those individuals who are unfamiliar with meditation techniques, and who therefore have no way of understanding or of controlling these symptoms in themselves. The other is that meditation itself is no chance response to a chance stimulus. It is a systematic and *willed* modulation of consciousness that puts the body into harmony with itself and with the macrocosm. The importance of this initiating element is clear in all ancient texts on Kuṇḍalinī and cannot be over-stressed.

There is a growing number of people in the West who are experiencing Kuṇḍalinī with much confusion, and turning to medical, psychiatric, parapsychological and new-age healing facilities which are not oriented to or experienced in the handling of the Kuṇḍalinī process. Many aspirants are concerned about the possibilities of dangers involved in the practice of self-taught kuṇḍalinī-yoga. It is true that a competent guru will help one to progress through a systematic method, yet responsibility must finally come back to oneself. One must learn to work with and control the inner energies.

* * *

Once experienced, the awakening of Kuṇḍalinī remains a permanent element in one's life. C. G. Jung points out: 'It is really a continuous development. It is not leaping up and down, for what you have arrived at is never lost. Say you have been in Mūlādhāra and then you reach the water-centre (Svādhisthāna), and afterwards you return, apparently. But you do not return; it is an illusion that you return; you have left something of yourself in the unconscious. Nobody touches the unconscious without leaving something of himself there. You may forget or repress it, you cannot lose the experience!'[38]

When the highest level is reached, the 'superconscious state' in which union is realized, one will eventually have to descend if one wants to express oneself through creativity; and when this creativity is completed, one will have the urge to return again into one's true identity, that is, to fusion with the Absolute.

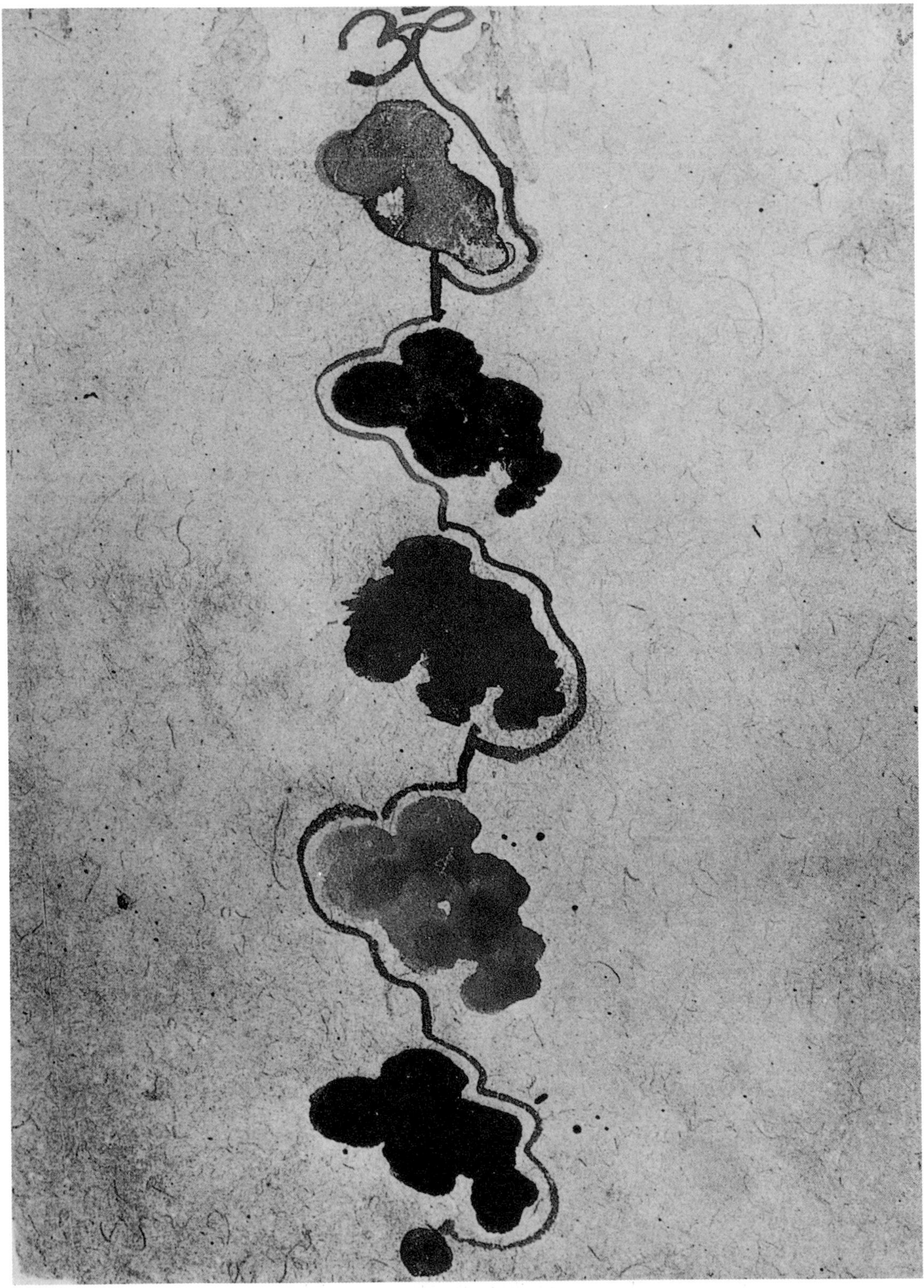

The ascending planes of consciousness from Mūlādhāra, earth, to Sahasrāra, union symbolized by the seed-mantra Oṃ

PURE TATTVAS

Macrocosmic Consciousness

MAHĀBINDU (VOID)

or

Nirguṇa Brahman ⬭ Paramaśiva

The Absolute/the Ultimate Reality

Śiva ⬭ Śakti

Pure Consciousness   Power Consciousness

Sat-Cit-Ānanda
Being-Consciousness-Bliss

Sadaśiva	Isvara	Suddhavidyā
Volition	Vibration	Action

↑ Involution

↓ Evolution

PSYCHICAL TATTVAS

Microcosmic Consciousness

Māyā Śakti
Objective plane of becoming

Sṛṣti	Sthiti	Pralaya (Samhāra)
Creation or emanation	Evolution or sustenance	Dissolution or reabsorption

generating a sense of difference by means of limiting principles, the five kañchukas or veilings

Kalā: partial manifestation/limitation of the universal consciousness

Vidyā: nescience, illusory knowledge of world-appearances

Rāga: power of selection, to discriminate between different frequencies

Kāla: operation of time space

Niyati: process of destiny

PHYSICAL TATTVAS

Material universe

Purusha ⬭⬭ Prakṛiti

Male Principle   Female Principle

GUṆAS

Constituents or qualities

Sattva	Rajas	Tamas
Essence	Movement	Inertia

Buddhi: intelligence
Ahamkāra: ego sense
Manas: mental functions

Jñanendriyas	Karmendriyas
Five sense organs	Five action organs
Ears: auditory, hearing	Mouth: speaking
Skin: tactile, feeling, touch	Hands: handling
Eyes: visual, seeing	Bowels: excreting
Tongue: gustatory, tasting	Genitals: sexual action
Nose: olfactory, smelling	Feet: locomotion

Tanmātras	Bhutas
Five subtle elements	Five gross elements
Energy of vibration: Śabda (sound as such)	Ether (Vyoman)
Energy of impact: Sparśa (touch as such)	Air (Marut)
Energy of light and form: Rūpa (form as such)	Fire (Tejas)
Energy of viscous attraction: Raśa (taste as such)	Water (Ap)
Energy of cohesive attraction: Gandha (smell as such)	Earth (Kṣiti)

Kuṇḍalini Energy System

NOTES ON THE TEXT

Sources for quotations from Sanskrit works are given within the text.

1, 36 Blair, *Rhythms of Vision*, pp. 8, 148-9.
2 Yogananda, *Autobiography of a Yogi*, p. 279.
3 Edwin Bernbaum, 'The Way of Symbols' in *The Journal of Transpersonal Psychology*, No. 2, 1974, pp. 99-100.
4 Schrader, *Introduction to the Pañcarātra*, p. 119.
5 Khanna, *Yantra*, p. 119.
6, 7, 8 Jung, *Psychological Commentary on Kundalini Yoga*, Lectures One, Two, Three and Four.
9 Chaudhuri, *Being, Evolution and Immortality*, pp. 193-4.
10, 11, 15 See for details: Mookerjee and Khanna, *The Tantric Way* (Ritual), pp. 175, 194.
12 Eliade, *Yoga, Immortality and Freedom*, pp. 270-1.
13 Vivekananda, *Rāja Yoga*, pp. 72-3.
14 Mishra, *Fundamentals of Yoga*, p. 104.
16 See Satyananda, *The Tantra of Kundalini Yoga*.
17, 19 Kenneth Ring, 'A Transpersonal View of Consciousness' in *The Journal of Transpersonal Psychology*, No. 2, 1977, pp. 148-9.
18 Stanislav Grof, 'LSD and the Cosmic Game' in *Journal for the Study of Consciousness*, 1972-3.
20 Gary E. Schwartz, 'The Current Findings on Physiology and Anxiety, Self-Control, Drug Abuse, and Creativity', paper presented at the American Psychological Association Convention, Montreal, August, 1973, p. 5.
21 Muktananda, *The Play of Consciousness*, pp. 90-9.
22 Gopi Krishna, *Kundalini*, pp. 64, 84, 87.
23 Prabhavananda, *The Spiritual Heritage of India*, p. 150
24 Saradananda, *Srī Ramakrishna, The Great Master*, p. 364, and see also the Advaita Āshram's *Life of Ramakrishna*, p. 108.
25 Dhyanyogi, *Light on Meditation*, p. 111.
26 Wilson, *The Outsider*, p. 268.
27 Kaviraj, *Sādhudarshan-O-Saṭprasaṅga*, Vol. I (in Bengali).
28 See Bentov, *Stalking the Wild Pendulum;* Bentov in Sannella, *Kundalini — Psychosis or Transcendence*.
29 Ken Wilber, 'Spectrum Psychology' in *Re-Vision*, Vol. 2, No. I, 1979, pp. 70-1.
30 Kaviraj, *Aspects of Indian Thought*, p. 234.
31, 32, 33, 37 Sannella, *Kundalini — Psychosis or Transcendence*.
34, 35 Tansley, *Radionics and the Subtle Anatomy of Man*, pp. 28, 23-4.
38 Jung, ibid, p. 18.

BIBLIOGRAPHY

Sanskrit sources

Darśana Upanishad
Dhyānabindu Upanishad
Gandharvatantra
Gheraṇḍa Saṁhitā
Haṭhayoga-pradīpikā
Jābālādarśana Upanishad
Jñana-Saṅkalini Tantra
Kāmadhenu Tantra
Kaṅkālīmālinī Tantra
Kulārnava Tantra
Lalitā-sahasranāma
Mahābhārata (Śānti-Parva)
Mahānirvāṇa Tantra
Mayā Tantra
Nādabindu Upanishad
Prapancasāra Tantra
Ratnasāra
Rudra-Yāmala
Śāṇḍilya Upanishad
Sāradātilaka
Ṣaṭcakra-nirūpaṇa
Ṣaṭcakra Upanishad
Saundaryalaharī
Siddha-Siddhānta-Paddhati
Śiva Saṁhitā
Svatantra Tantra
Varāha Upanishad
Yoga Kuṇḍalinī Upanishad
Yoga Sūtra of Patañjali
Yogavāsistha Rāmāyaṇa

Others works

Arundale, G. S., *Kundalini: An Occult Experience,* Madras 1974.

Banerjea, A. K., *Philosophy of Goraknāth with Goraksha-Vacana-Saṅgraha,* Gorakhpur 1963.

Bentov, Itzhak, *Stalking the Wild Pendulum,* New York 1977.

Blair, Lawrence, *Rhythms of Vision,* London 1975.

Capra, Fritjof, *The Tao of Physics,* Boulder 1975.

Chaudhuri, Haridas, *Being, Evolution and Immortality,* Wheaton 1974.

Das, Upendrakumar, *Bhāratiya Śaktisādhanā,* Vols. I and II (in Bengali), Calcutta, Bengali date 1373.

Datta, M. R., *The Secret Serpent,* Dacca 1913.

Dhyanyogi, Madhusudandas, *Light on Meditation,* Los Angeles 1978.

Eliade, Mircea, *Yoga, Immortality and Freedom,* London 1958, Princeton 1973.

Gopi Krishna, *Kundalini, the evolutionary energy in man,* Boulder and London 1971.

Goswami, Shyam Sundar, *Layayoga,* London 1980.

Jung, C. G., *Psychological Commentary on Kundalini Yoga,* Lectures One, Two, Three and Four, 1932 (from the Notes of Mary Foote), published in *Spring,* New York, 1975-6.

Kashmir Shaivaism, Research and Publication Department, Govt. of Jammu and Kashmir, Srinagar 1962.

Kaviraj, Gopinath, *Sādhudarshan-O-Satprasaṇga,* Vol. I. (in Bengali), Calcutta, Bengali date 1369.

——, *Aspects of Indian Thought,* Burdwan University, West Bengal 1966.

Khanna, Madhu, *Yantra,* London and New York 1979.

Kundalini, Evolution and Enlightenment, ed. John White, New York 1979.

Leadbeater, C. W., *The Chakras,* Madras 1966, London 1972, Wheaton 1977.

Life of Śrī Rāmakrishna, published by the Advaita Ashram, Calcutta 1977.

Mishra, Rammurti S., *Fundamentals of Yoga,* New York 1974.

Mookerjee, Ajit, *Tantra Asana,* Basel, New York etc., 1971.

——, *Yoga Art,* London, New York etc, 1975.

——, and Madhu Khanna, *The Tantric Way,* London, New York etc, 1977.

Muktananda, Swami, *The Play of Consciousness,* San Francisco 1974.

——, *Kundalini,* So. Fallsburg, N. Y. 1979.

Narayananda, Swami, *The Primal Power in Man,* Rishikesh 1950.

Nikhilaṅanda, Swami, *Hinduism,* London 1959.

——, *The Gospel of Rāmakrishna,* tr., New York 1974.

Pandit, M. P., *Kundalini Yoga,* Madras 1959.

Prabhavananda, Swami, *The Spiritual Heritage of India,* London 1962, New York 1963.

Pratyagatmananda Saraswati, Swami, and Sir John Woodroffe, *Sadhana for Self-Realization,* Madras 1963.

Radha, Swami Sivananda, *Kundalini,* Spokane 1978.

Rai, A. K., *Kundalini the Goddess,* Calcutta 1908.

Rajneesh, Bhagvan Shree. *The Books of the Secrets*, Poona 1976.
Rele, Vasant G., *The Mysterious Kundalini*, Bombay *1960*.
Rendel, Peter, *Introduction to the Chakras*, Wellingborough 1977.
Sannella, Lee, *Kundalini — Psychosis or Transcendence*, San Francisco 1977.
Saradananda, Swami, *Śrī Ramakrishna, The Great Master*, Madras, n.d.
Satcakra (Sanskrit with Bengali commentary), ed. H. Devasharmana, Calcutta, n.d.
Satyananda Saraswati, Swami, *Tantra of Kundalini Yoga*, Monghyr 1973.
Schrader, F. Otto, *Introduction to the Pañcarātra and Ahirbudhnya Saṁhitā*, Madras 1916.
Singh, Jaidev, *Śiva Sūtras*, Varanasi 1979.
——, *Pratyabhijñahrdayam*, tr., Delhi 1963.
Singh, L. P., *Tantra*, New Delhi 1976.
Sivananda Sarasvati, Swami, *Kundalini Yoga*, Rishikesh 1950.
Tansley, David V., *Radionics and The Subtle Anatomy of Man*, Bradford 1976.
Varenne, Jean, *Yoga and the Hindu Tradition*, Chicago and London 1976.
Vishnu Tirtha, Swami, *Devātmā Shakti (Kuṇḍalinī)*, Rishikesh 1962.
Vivekananda, Swami, *Rāja Yoga*, Calcutta 1962.
Walker, Benjamin, *Hindu World*, Vols I and II, London 1963.
Wilson, Colin, *The Outsider*, London 1978.
Woodroffe, Sir John (Arthur Avalon), *The Serpent Power*, New York 1978.
Yogananda, Paramahansa, *Autobiography of a Yogi*, Los Angeles 1977.
Yoga Upanishads (The), tr. T. R. S. Ayyangar, Madras 1952.
Yogeshananda, Swami, *The Visions of Śrī Ramakṛishṇa*, Madras, n.d.
Zukav, Gary, *The Dancing Wu Li Masters (An Overview of the New Physics)*, New York 1979.

GLOSSARY

ABHAYA, an upright mudrā, the hand-gesture of dispelling fear, giving protection and bestowing benediction.

ABSOLUTE, the Supreme Reality; the transcendent divine principle.

ADHIKĀRA, prerogative, spiritual authority.

AGNI, the fire-god; one of the gross elements of the physical world: fire.

AIRĀVATA, the celestial white elephant with six trunks, vehicle of the Vedic god Indra.

ĀJÑĀ, meaning 'command', the sixth chakra, situated between the eyebrows in the subtle body. A major chakra, the centre at which consciousness goes 'transpersonal'.

ĀKĀŚA, region of pure consciousness, etheric space, the subtlest of the five cosmic elements, associated with the fifth chakra Viśuddha which controls the principle of sound.

ANĀHATA, meaning 'unstruck'; the heart chakra in the subtle body.

ĀNANDA, transcendent bliss, the essential principle of joy, spiritual ecstasy.

ĀNANDAMAYA (kośa), the most subtle 'bliss-formed' sheath (kośa) of the causal body, the sphere of the all-transcendent blissful consciousness.

ANANTA, meaning 'endless', serpent, often identified with Śesha, another Great Nāga (nāga = serpent), whose thousands heads fan out into a mighty hood, forming the couch of Vishnu who reclines on his coils in trance-sleep, an archetype of the unconscious.

ANNAMAYA-KOŚA, the 'food-formed' sheath of the 'gross' body (sthūla śarīra), made up of five gross elements, or bhūta — earth, water, fire, air, ether — which are resolved again into their initial states after death.

ANUSVĀRA, an extended nasalized sound of the Sanskrit alphabet; an unpronounceable 'vibration' capable of articulation in conjunction with a letter of the alphabet; represented as a semi-circle in which a dot symbolizing the bindu is inserted.

APĀNA, one of the prāṇic energies that moves downwards, controlling the vital air in the lower abdominal region: a downward wind linked with the fire element.

ARDHACANDRA, a sound-level above the Ājñā chakra. In the gradual elimination of differentiation experienced by the adept, on the sonic level upward from the Ājñā chakra, the Ardhacandra resonance is symbolized by the half moon (see p. 89).

ARDHVANĀRĪŚVARA, an androgynous form of Śiva-Śakti, having the characteristics of both male and female in one body. Every man and every woman contains within himself or herself both male and female principles.

ĀSANAS, postures of the body, yogic poses, establishing balance and poise.

AŚVANI, a mudrā (or bandha = 'knot') consisting of the contraction of internal organs to seal the occult orifices of the body and bring vital centres under control; performance of secret 'internal' acts while the yogic posture is steadily maintained.

BĀNA-LINGA *see* liṅga

BANARAS, or Vārānasī, one of the holy cities of India, situated on the Ganges.

BANDHAS, meaning 'knots', muscular contractions sometimes included in the yogic mudrās or āsanas. Among the important bandhas, in which one is locked in a contracted position, are Mūla-bandha, 'root contraction', Jālandhara, 'net-holding', Uḍḍiyāna, 'flying'.

BHAIRAVĪ, a female guru. It is considered ideal to be initiated by a Bhairavī. Tantrikas perform group rituals of sexo-yogic āsanas known as chakra-pūjā or 'circle-worship', of which Bhairavī-chakra is the most important.

BHAKTI-YOGA, realization through love and devotion; intense desire and will for union with one's chosen deity.

BHŪTA-ŚUDHI, purification of the gross physical element during ritual.

BĪJA-MANTRA, a nuclear seed-sound syllable symbolizing a deity or cosmic force.

BINDU, metaphysical point. The compact mass of śakti, energy, absorbed into an undifferentiated point ready for creation.

BRAHMĀ, the Creator, Brahmā is associated in Hindu cosmology with the creation of the universe.

BRAHMĀ KNOT, a psychic blockage in the subtle body. To clear this knot at the time of the rising of Kuṇḍalinī is to get established in totality.

BRAHMA-NĀḌĪ, the central psychic channel, Sushumṇā, through which the ascent of Kuṇḍalinī takes place.

BRAHMAN, the ultimate Reality, Pure Consciousness that is the unchanging principle of all changes.

BRĀHMAṆĪ, the female guru of Ramakrishna (1836-

1886), the great saint of nineteenth-century India.

BRAHMA-RANDHRA, the Sahasrāra chakra, situated just above the crown of the head, where Kuṇḍalinī, Power Consciousness, unites with Pure Consciousness.

CHAITANYA, Pure Consciousness. It is the goal of the individual consciousness to merge itself in the Cosmic Consciousness in Universal Bliss.

CHĀKINĪ ŚAKTI, or Rākinī Śakti, is the power of Vishṇu, the presiding deity of the Svādhisthāna chakra.

CHAKRAS (or cakras), literally 'wheels' or 'circles', the term used for the psychic centres of energy situated along the spinal column in the subtle body of the human organism, generally symbolized by lotuses.

CHAKRA-PŪJĀ, literally, 'circle-worship', the group ritual of union, performed collectively by a circle of Tantric initiates. The rite is designated Pañcha-makāra, or 'five M's', for the five ingredients used in worship.

CHITRIṆĪ, one of the subtle channels within the Sushumṇā nāḍī, the main channel which runs up from the root chakra Mūlādhāra.

CIT-ŚAKTI, Consciousness as power, the supreme energy, the female counterpart of Śiva as Pure Consciousness.

COSMIC CONSCIOUSNESS *see* Chaitanya

COSMIC CYCLE, the sequence of yugas. India does not think in terms of historical time, but conceives of time as cyclical, through the doctrine of 'yugas' or ages. A complete cosmic cycle consists of four successive ages of varying length. At the end of each mahā-yuga, the world is dissolved in a cosmological event known as laya, or dissolution, in order to manifest again. This phase is known as sṛṣṭi, emanation or creation, and is followed by a phase called sthiti, evolution or preservation; and then by saṃhāra, 'dissolution' — a continuous cycle of cosmic events.

COSMIC MAN, the original primeval man known as Purusha. A counterpart is the primeval female Virāj, also termed Prakṛiti, or Nature.

ḌĀKINĪ, the 'energy' (śakti) of the presiding deity Brahmā of the root centre, Mūlādhāra chakra.

DAKSHIṆĀCHĀRA, the 'right-hand' tantric practice of Pañcha-makāra, in which the five 'ingredients' are used metaphorically. Madya (wine), literally drunk in 'left-hand' practice, is represented by coconut milk, as the symbol of 'intoxicating knowledge'; māṁsa (meat) for which ginger or radish is substituted, implies the control of speech (from the word *ma*, meaning tongue); for matsya (fish), there is concentration on the two vital currents in the Iḍā and Piṅgalā (subtle channels on each side of the central subtle channel Sushumnā); mudrā (parched cereal) is eaten in both left-hand and right-hand practice, and symbolizes the yogic state of concentration; for maithuna (sexual union) two kinds of flowers are used, representing liṅga and yoni, to symbolize meditation upon the primal act of creation.

DAKSHIṆA MĀRGA *see* Dakshiṇāchāra

ETHERIC DOUBLE, the subtle body. It is believed that human body, within its corporeal frame, embraces all the subtle planes of the universe; beyond one's physical existence there is a parallel 'etheric double' which constitutes one's subtle body. The subtle sheaths are related to the gross body at several psychic points.

FEMALE PARTICIPANT Partner in performing sexo-yogic ritual who is considered the reflection of Śakti, and plays the role of divine Energy, without which the practice of tantric āsana cannot be successful.

FEMALE PRINCIPLE, the 'devout woman', epitomizes the entire nature of femaleness, the essence of all the śaktis in their various aspects. Śakti is the female principle or the dynamic aspect of the Ultimate Reality, the energy that permeates all creation.

GRANTHIS, psychic knots. The three chakras Mūlādhāra, Anāhata and Ājñā are associated with the Brahmā, Vishṇu and Rudra knots respectively, and with psychic blockages called liṅgas — the Svayaṁbhu, Bāṇa and Itara liṅgas — which are to be surmounted in the passage of the rising Kuṇḍalinī.

GURU, a spiritual preceptor. The esoteric truths can only be transmitted by an experienced teacher who has the authority to initiate the disciple into the various techniques to attain enlightenment.

HA, the symbol of Śakti, while 'A' is the symbol of Śiva.

HĀKINĪ, or Siddhakālī, the 'energy' of the presiding deity Paramaśiva of the Ajñā chakra.

HAṂ, the seed mantra of the Viśuddha chakra.

HAṬHA-YOGA, a method of developing psychosomatic forces, chiefly by means of control of the body and its powers and functions. The syllable *ha* represents the sun, *tha* the moon, and these together symbolize the polarity in each human being, Hatha-yoga prescribes eight stages to the attainment of the ultimate goal: (1) yama, restraint (2) niyama, internal control, (3) āsana, body-posture, (4) prānāyāma, breath control (5) pratyāhāra, control of the sense, (6) dhārana, meditation, (7) dhyāna, contemplation and (8) samādhi, a trance-like state.

HIMĀLAYAS, from 'hima-ālaya', 'snow-abode', the mighty range of mountains which plays an important part in Indian history, mythology, art and religion. The 'rishies' or sages, yogis and saints credited with universal knowledge or esoteric powers had their contemplative retreats in the Himālayas.

IḌĀ, the white, 'lunar' subtle channel or nāḍī, coiling round the central channel, the Sushumṇā, and ending at the left nostril.

INDRA, the most celebrated god of the *Ṛig Veda*. His worship probably coincides with a phase of Aryan expansion into the hinterland of India.

ITARA LIṄGA *see* liṅga

KĀKINĪ ŚAKTI, the 'energy' of the presiding deity Ishā of the Anāhata chakra, the heart centre.

KĀLĪ, the divine Śakti, representing the creative and destructive aspects of nature. Kālī is the symbol of the dynamic power of eternal Time (Kāla), and in this aspect she signifies annihilation through which the seed of life emerges. She inspires terror and love at the same time.

KARMA-YOGA, yoga of action through which one can attain liberation.

KHECHARĪ, meaning 'air-moving', a mudrā consisting of turning the tongue backwards into the throat, blocking the orifice of the nasal passages so that the 'nectar' flowing down from the Sahāsrāra after the rise of Kuṇḍalinī is arrested.

KOŚAS, sheaths. A human being is conceived of as having a number of sheaths, or kośas, that is, layers of decreasing density.

KRISHṆA, the most celebrated deity of the Hindu pantheon. The *Bhagavadgītā* expresses his doctrine.

KRIYĀ, the path of 'action'.

KUMBHAKA, retention of the breath for a period at any point during inhalation.

KUṆḌALINĪ (also Kuṇḍalinī-Śakti, Kula-kuṇḍalinī, Fire Kuṇḍalinī, Sun Kuṇḍalinī, Moon Kuṇḍalinī, physio-kundalini), the cosmic female energy (śakti) in Mūlādhāra chakra. The manifested Kuṇḍalinī becomes Kula, an all-transcending light of consciousness; from Mūlādhāra to Anāhata, Fire Kuṇḍalinī; from Anāhata to Viśuddha, Sun Kuṇḍalinī; from Viśuddha to the end of Sushumṇā-nāḍī, Moon Kuṇḍalinī. The various disciplines practised for the arousal of Kuṇḍalinī, and for consciousness-expanding experience, are known as kuṇḍalinī-yoga. Western researchers into the phenomenon have proposed a 'physio-kundalini' model to account for their observations.

KŪRMA, tortoise, the sacred incarnation of Vishṇu. The form assumed by him during the Churning of the Ocean to extract the immortal nectar.

LĀKINĪ ŚAKTI, the 'energy' of the deity Rudra associated with Maṇipūra chakra.

LAṂ, the seed mantra of Mūlādhāra chakra, the root centre at the base of the spine.

LAYA, laya-yoga, 'absorption', whose goal is the merging of the individual consciousness with the divine object of one's contemplation.

LIṄGA (also Svayaṁbhu-liṅga, Bāṇa-liṅga, Itara liṅga, liṅgam), exoteric meaning, phallus; esoteric meaning, subtle space in which the whole universe is in the process of formation and dissolution: *li*, to dissolve, and *gam*, to go out, to evolve. The Svayaṁbhu, Bāṇa and Itara liṅgas are psychic blockages that are to be surmounted in kuṇḍalinī-yoga.

LOTUS PETALS, the usual symbolic representation of the chakras. The Sanskrit letters inscribed on their (specified) number of petals indicate sound-vibrations representing the varying intensities of the energies working in the different chakras.

M: madya, māṁsa, matsya, mudrā, maithuna, the five ingredients of the Pañcha-makāra (five M's). Followers of the left-hand rite employ the five ingredients literally. *See also* Chakra-pūjā, Dakshiṇāchāra.

MADHYAMĀ, cosmic sound in its subtle form, prior to its gross manifestation.

MAHĀBINDU, the supersonic and metacosmic Void. According to Kashmir Śaivism, the ultimate Reality is Pure Consciousness, i.e., Paramaśiva or Parābindu or Mahābindu.

MAHĀMUDRĀ, sexo-yogic āsana known as the 'great posture', in which the practitioner sits with the left heel pressed against the perineum (yoni-place) and the right leg stretched out, while holding the right foot with both hands.

MAKARA, an animal symbol, a sea-monster resembling a crocodile, associated with Svādhisthāna chakra.

MAṆIPŪRA, the third chakra, at the level of the solar plexus, related to the element fire.

MANOMAYA, a sheath of discriminatory process (*see also* Kośas).

MANTRA, mantra śakti, sacred sound, based on the

principle that sound has power, śakti. It induces manana, or reflection of the Ultimate, and provides trāṇa, or protection for the transmigratory life.

MATSYA *see* M

MĀYĀ, the veiling of Reality by the differentiation and limitation of the phenomenal world.

MUDRĀ, yogic gesture or posture.

MŪLĀDHĀRA, the root chakra at the base of the spine, in the subtle body.

NĀDA, cosmic sound approaching manifestation. Anāhata nād is the 'unstruck' sound experienced in Sushumṇā.

NĀDĀNTA, creative pulsation of sound and light. Dr Jaidev Singh explains in *Śiva Sūtras* (a Kashmir Śaiva text, p.xii) that from the intensive awareness of the ultimate sound, praṇava (Oṃ), there follow nine stages of yoga, experiences of subtle forms of sound, nāda, known as nine nādas (see p. 89). The first 'vision' is bindu (1), known as Ardha mātrā. The next is Ardhacandra (2), subtler than the previous stage. Each succeeding stage is subtler than the last: Rodhinī (3), Nāda (4), Nādānta (5), Śakti (6), Vyāpinī (7), Samanā (or Nirvāṇa) (8), Unmanā or Unmanī (9). Unmanī is the highest aspect of consciousness. Up to Samanā, there can be only realization of the essential Self (ātma-vyāpti). It is only at the stage of Unmanī that there can be, not only the realization of the metaphysical Self, but also the realization of the world as an aspect of Self (Śiva-vyāpti). Kṣemarāja (a tenth-century commentator) remarks (in sūtra seven of the third section of the *Śiva-sūtras*) that up to Unmanī, there is the play of māyā, the veiling of reality by differentiation and limitation. It is only at the stage of Unmanī that māyā ceases completely.

NĀḌĪS, the channels of the subtle body, through which the vital, prāṇic and astral currents flow.

NĀRĀYAṆA, a name of Vishṇu, derived from either *nara*, the original primeval man, or from *nāra*, the Cosmic Waters, the place of motion.

NĀTHA YOGIS, 'lord' yogis who rose to prominence in Northern India during the tenth century AD, and whose saints bear the title of Nātha. Nātha yogis were usually Śaivites (followers of Śiva), and developed a yogic body-language, thereby attaining supernatural powers.

NIRVĀṆA *see* Nādānta

NYĀSA, an 'empathy building' method which expands the awareness. In the tantra ritual known as Nyāsa, parts of the body are sensitized by placing the fingertips on sensory-awareness zones.

OJAS, Ojas śakti, energy (śakti), a vital force, the quintessence of all bodily substances, pervading the whole body and important for psychic potency.

OṂ (A-U-M), the most powerful of all seed-sound syllables and the source of all mantras. A key to realization.

PADMĀSANA, 'padma' meaning 'lotus', yogic posture in which one sits with legs crossed, right foot placed on left thigh, left foot crossed over on right leg, soles of feet turned upwards, with hands holding the toes.

PAÑCHA-MAKĀRA *see* M

PARĀ, unmanifested sound; the highest stage of consciousness.

PARĀBINDU *see* Mahābindu

PARAMAŚIVA *see* Mahābindu

PASHYANTĪ, sound emerging towards the audible and transmitted by reverberation.

PATAÑJALI, the Sanskrit grammarian (*c.* 300 BC) and compiler of the earliest systematic treatises on yoga. Patañjali's sūtras are divided into four, dealing with samādhi, yoga discipline, psychic powers and liberation (Kaivalya).

PIṄGALĀ, the solar subtle channel on the right side of the body.

PRAKṚITI, Nature, the creative energy, the source of objectivity, the primeval female principle, counterpart of Purusha (see p. 99).

PRAṆA, prāṇa-śakti, the vital air of the inner body, the life-force, or śakti, energy.

PRĀṆAYĀMA, meaning 'breath-way', yogic breathing which plays a vital part in meditative exercises.

PRĀṆAMAYA-KOŚA, a sheath (kośa) in the subtle body through which the vital energy circulates.

PRAṆAVA, ultimate sound, Oṃ, originating creation.

PURAKA, one of the four breathing processes, 'filling' or inhalation, shallow or deep.

PURUSHA, the first principle in Sāṁkhya philosophy. Generally represents the eternal Cosmic Spirit, the counterpart of the female principle. Prakṛiti (see p. 99).

RĀJA-YOGA, 'royal' yoga whch emphasizes mental and spiritual rather than physical culture. Its aim is to make one a 'ruler' over all one's mental and spiritual equipment.

RĀKINĪ *see* Chākinī

RAM, the seed syllable of the Manipūra chakra.

RECHAKA, exhalation of breath, which may be shallow or full.

RODHINĪ *see* Mahābindu

RUDRA, originally a Vedic god of many aspects. Later

mythology associated Rudra with the god Śiva.

RUDRA KNOT, psychic blockage at the Ājñā chakra. To clear the Rudra knot in kuṇḍalinī-yoga is to attain the non-dual state, the realization of oneness.

ŚABDA-BRAHMAMAYĪ, Śakti as the ultimate Reality, in the form of primal sound-energy.

SADĀŚIVA, the presiding deity of the Viśuddha chakra, as the androgynous aspect of Śiva; also the third tattva (see p. 99) counting from Śiva as the ultimate Reality.

SĀDHAKA, a spiritual aspirant, seeker, one who is disciplined.

SĀDHANĀ, spiritual discipline.

'SĀ 'HAṀ, I am She' and 'So 'ham, I am He', phrase identifying one's own essential nature, 'So 'ham', with the ultimate Reality.

SAHAJOLI, a secret mudrā. Sahaja means 'co-born'. The yogi draws up the female 'seed' through his organ and brings it into his own body.

SAHASRĀRA, the highest psychic centre, above the crown of the head, symbolized by the thousand-petalled lotus. The place where Kuṇḍalinī unites with Śiva, Pure Consciousness.

ŚAIVĀGAMA, Śaiva-Āgamas, texts expounding the doctrines of Śiva, known as sāstras. There are ten dualistic treatises, eighteen that teach identity in differences, and sixty-four non-dualistic treatises.

SĀKINĪ, the 'energy' presiding over the Viśuddha chakra located in the subtle body.

ŚAKTI, the dynamic aspect of the Ultimate Principle, the power that permeates all creation, the energy of Śiva the foundational consciousness.

ŚAKTI-CHĀLANĀS, energy-movers.

ŚAKTIPĀT, kuṇḍalinī-yoga, the path through which Kuṇḍalinī ascends.

SAMĀDHI, enstasis, a trance-like state in which the fluctuation of the mind ceases; the last stage of yoga in whch the final identification is reached.

SAMĀNA, one of the vital airs of Prāṇa, in the navel area, believed to be white or green in colour.

SAṂHĀRA, the withdrawal or reabsorption of the universe into the original Ground.

SĀṀKHYA-YOGA, one of the earliest systems of Hindu philosophy, founded by the sage Kapila. It postulates two uncaused ultimate Realities, Purusha and Prakṛiti, the male and female principles. The twenty-five tattvas or categories formulated by it are regarded as transformations resulting from the inter-operation of these two principles. The three guṇas (qualities) of the categories — sattva (essence), rajas (movement) and tamas (inertia) — make up Pṛakriti's manifestation of the material universe (see p. 99).

SAMSARA, the world-process in its transmigratory existence.

SAMSKĀRA, an imprinted impression or fruit of karmic action.

ŚESHA, 'residue', a serpent so named because of its birth after the creation of the Three Worlds. Its great coils and mighty hood of serpent-power symbolize eternity, the depths of the unconscious.

SEXO-YOGIC ĀSANA, ritual and discipline for the spiritualization of sex, and the transformation of its energy to the mental plane. The āsana ritual is free from emotional impulses. It is sustained by the technical possibility of using sex energy as a medium of arousing Kuṇḍalinī for ultimate realization.

SIDDHĀSANA, from 'siddha', 'attainment', one of the most important yogic postures in which one sits upright on the left heel and crosses the right foot over the left ankle. The āsana directs the mind towards realization.

ŚIVA, Hindu god. In esoteric meaning, Śiva is Pure Consciousness, the transcendent divine principle.

SONIC CONSCIOUSNESS, ultimate Reality in the form of primal Sound.

SPHOTA, the eternal sound element, pure and unmanifested, the creative principle of the universe.

SṚṢṬI, creation, or emanation, one of the three aspects of the world-process. The others are sthiti, evolution or maintenance, and pralaya or saṃhāra, dissolution or reabsorption into the original state in order to emanate again (see p. 99).

STHŪLA ŚARĪRA, the gross physical body.

SŪKŚMA, sūkśma śarīra, the subtle body, in which the different psychic centres, the chakras, are located.

SUPREME MAN *see* Cosmic Man

SUSHUMṆĀ, the central subtle channel through which Kuṇḍalinī rises in the human body.

SŪTRAS, ancient metaphysical and philosophical texts.

SVĀDHISTHĀNA, the second chakra, next to the root chakra Mūlādhāra, in the region above the genitals.

SVAYAṀBHU-LIṄGA *see* liṅga

TANMĀTRAS, categories, the primary elements of perception, the particulars of sense-perception: śabda (sound), sparśa (touch), rūpa (form), raśa (taste), gandha (smell). See p. 99.

TANTRA-ĀSANA *see* sexo-yogic āsana

TANTRA-YOGA-ĀSANA *see* sexo-yogic āsana

TANTRIKAS, those who follow the discipline of tantra.

TATTVAS, the subtle and material elements of the universe, 'thatness', cosmic categories (see p. 99).

THIRD EYE, the point in the middle of the forehead, between the eyebrows, where cosmic consciousness opens.

UDĀNA, one of the vital airs of Prāṇa, in the throat region, believed to be pale blue in colour.

UḌḌIYĀNA, 'flying', a mudrā in which one alternately contracts and relaxes the abdominal muscles, rapidly changing from side to side, 'like quivering water'.

UDGĪTHA, the 'ultimate song'.

UNMANĪ *see* Nādānta

ŪRDHVARETA, sexo-yogic exercise. 'Reta' has the esoteric meaning of two substances, sukra or semen (white in colour) and rakta (red in colour). The emission of these vital energies must be controlled. Through tantric practices, sexual power can be regulated, arresting the retas. The technique of this is known as 'ūrdha-reta', 'upward-flow', and converts the retas into vital energy and gives it an upward direction without wastage.

VAJRA, thunderbolt. Held by the deities of the chakras, weapons such as the vajra are for conquering the ego and the senses, as if in war.

VAJROLI, from vajra, 'thunderbolt', an important mudrā to control and regulate the sexual energy of the body.

VAIKHARĪ, the fourth stage of sound, gross physical sound or vibration, manifesting as the word.

VAṂ, the seed-mantra of the Svādhisthāna chakra.

VĀMĀCHĀRA *see* M

VĀMA MĀRGA *see* M

VARA, a mudrā (hand-gesture) granting boons.

VARĀHA, Vishṇu in the form of a boar, his third evolutionary incarnation.

VARUṆA, Vedic deity, Lord of the Ocean, originally conceived as the sustainer of the universe, the deity presiding over *ṛita,* the order of the cosmos.

VĀYU, 'air', Vedic deity, god of winds.

VEDIC, the Indo-European language in which the *Vedas*, sacred scriptures, were composed. The *Ṛig Veda* is the most ancient literature of the Vedic Age, *c.* 1500 BC.

VIJÑĀNAMAYA, the intelligence sheath in the subtle body.

VISHṆU, one of the most important gods of the Hindu pantheon. By the time of the *Mahābhārata,* he emerges as a god of paramount importance, and the second god of the Hindu triad, being regarded as the Preserver, just as Brahmā is the Creator and Śiva the Destroyer.

VISHṆU KNOT, the psychic blockage associated with the fourth chakra, Anāhata.

VIŚUDDHA, the fifth chakra, in the throat region.

VOID *see* Mahābindu

VYĀPIKĀ *see* Nādānta

YAJÑA, sacrifice, one of the main pillars of the Vedic ritual system, an essential condition of salvation.

YAṂ, the seed mantra of the Anāhata chakra.

YAMA, the first stage of yoga which restrains and controls the physical.

YOGIN, student of yoga; feminine: yoginī.

YONI, the primal root or source of objectivization. Symbolized by a triangle pointing downwards. The female sex organs, symbol of cosmic mysteries.

YONI ĀSANA, a secret yoga posture generally taught by the guru.

YONI-MUDRĀ, preparation in which the adept is required to sit in Siddhāsana, contracting the yoni-place between the sex-organs and the anus.

INDEX

Page numbers in italics indicate illustrations, roman numerals refer to colour plates

Acknowledgments

Illustrations (monochrome identified by page numbers, colour by roman numerals) are drawn from the following collections:
Archaeological Survey of India, New Delhi, 58
Achim Bedrich, Munich, 18
C. L. Bharany, New Delhi, X, XI, 77, XIV
Bharat Kala Bhavan, Banares, 50-1, 57, VIII
Boroda Museum, Boroda, 31
British Library, London, III
Bala Chowdhury, London (photograph), 60
J.C. Ciancimino, London, 6, 13, 55
Alex Grey, Boston, 12
Christina Grof, Big Sur, 91
Stanislaus Klossowski, I
Ajit Mookerjee, 8, 13, 14, 16, 22 (photograph Eileen Tweedy), 23, 24, 34-5, 36-7, 38, V, VI, 52, 53, 56, IX, 97, 98
B. Sharma, New Delhi, 63
R.C. Sharma, Jaipur, 53
Arturo Schwarz, Milan, 44, 81, 82
Hans Wichers, Hamburg, VII, XV, XVI
Jan Wichers, Hamburg (photographs Tokyo Gallery, Tokyo), 2, 15, 17, II, IV, XII, 69, 70, XIII
Temple plan, 60, after Cunningham.